Let this book help serve as your starting point for creating the life you want.
Now is the time to step up and set a new standard!

You Are Awesome!

Published 2009
Printed by Success Press Publishing in the United States of America

ISBN 978-0-9824319-0-0

This book is available at quantity
discounts for bulk purchases.
For information, please call 1-877-803-4221.

FOR STUDENT SUCCESS

How to Get Started When You Don't Know Where to Begin

Arel Moodie

DEDICATION

To my loving grandmother.

Even though you left this earth before I

was able to share this book with you,

I know you are looking down at me

from above. I hope I made you proud.

RIP Madge Moodie

(September 23, 1918–May 5, 2009)

ACKNOWLEDGMENTS

This book is a dream come true for me. However, I am well aware there is no possible way I could ever have done this on my own. There are so many people to thank, and I know I am probably going to forget someone. Please know that if I do, it is a mistake of my head and not of my heart.

I'd like to first thank G-d for all that has been provided for me and the lessons I learn every day.

To the love of my life, Yolanda Febles, I would be nothing if I never met you.

To my brother, Moise Moodie, you are the rock of my life and my source of strength. To my mother, Janice, who has loved and supported me throughout my entire life. To my father, Warren, who has been the biggest role model in my life and the person who has taught me how to be a man and a leader. I hope you all understand how much I truly am grateful that you are in my life.

To my aunts, uncles, grandparents, and cousins, thank you for your support and love throughout my entire life.

To Bert Gervais, your friendship is one of the most valuable things I have on this earth. To Adrian Scotland, thank you for helping me develop my confidence and dance skills. To Michael Simmons and Sheena Lindahl, thank you for being such awesome mentors and friends. To Patricia Hudak, thank you for holding me accountable to my goals. You are all rare and true friends.

Melissa Caron, thank you for all of your help designing the book. To my editors Kristin Walinski and Debbie Feldstein, thank you for helping turn my ideas into a coherent book.

To Victor Antonio, thank you for giving me the inspiration I needed to pursue my dreams as a professional speaker and to write this book. To Angelo Mastrangelo, thank you for being my mentor and confidant when I was just a kid in a classroom with a dream.

To the Slonims, Harkavys, Creegers, and Dani Schon, thank you for all of your spiritual guidance.

To all the students and educators who bring me in to speak every year, you are the reason I do what I do.

And to you, thank you for taking the time to read this book. I look forward to hearing about your journey.

PRAISE FOR YOUR STARTING POINT FOR STUDENT SUCCESS

"Arel's principles are simple yet extremely effective. His book will show you how to create success in your life where and when it really counts."

- T. Harv Eker, Author of #1 NY Times Bestseller
  Secrets of the Millionaire Mind

"There are many books out there that claim to know what they are talking about but Arel's message is the real deal. Every student needs to read this book."

- Jonathan Sprinkles,
  former National Campus Speaker of the Year
  www.jsprinkles.com

"Arel's message is genuine and heartfelt, but most importantly it is the best investment you can make in starting your journey to success. You can't afford not to read this book!"

- Cameron Johnson,
  TV Personality and Author of You Call the Shots

"As someone who knows what it takes to create success from the inside out, I recommend Arel's principles to any student what wants to start on their own journey to success."

- Ephren W. Taylor II, Youngest African America CEO of a Publicly Traded Company, Celebrity Entrepreneur & Bestselling Author of Creating Success From the Inside Out

" Want to understand how to align what you LOVE with what you DO and live a passionate life? Read this book now. Don't put it down."

- Ryan Allis, best-selling author of Zero to One Million and CEO of iContact Corp.

" If you are a student that is ready to make your dreams a reality, this book will help you get there and get there fast!"

- Michael Simmons, author of the bestselling book The Student Success Manifesto

"It's easy to talk about being successful, but harder to live a life based upon proven principles of excellence. In a genuine and heartfelt way, Arel will teach you how to do just that. The strategies he shares will resonate with you long after finish reading and you'll feel compelled to pay forward what you just learned with others."

- David Coleman, "The Dating Doctor" and "America's Real-Life Hitch!," 12-time National College Speaker of the Year

"Every so often I meet an extraordinary individual whose unique perspective re-energizes and re-ignites our passion for success in all things. If you're feeling stuck or frustrated, Arel's book is a great 'starting point' to get you going!"

- Victor Antonio, author of The L.O.G.I.C of Success, College Diversity Speaker of the Year

"This book is powerful! As a leadership coach, I must encourage you to go out and read this book, and pick up several copies for your friends and family members. It's gonna knock your socks off!"

- Bea Fields, Co-Author of Millennial Leaders and EDGE! A Leadership Story

"You must read and re-read the "life changing moment" in chapter 2. Arel's ability to speak with conviction and candor about his personal challenges are awe-inspiring."

- Bertrand Gervais, Author of Who's In Your Top Hive? and CEO The Place Finder LLC

"If I had this book as a student I would have graduated with honors and escaped the maze of mediocrity with a ridiculous head-start on the competition."

- Al Duncan: The Millennial Mentor™
World-Class Professional Speaker - www.alduncan.net

TABLE OF CONTENTS

CHAPTER ONE

INTRODUCTION

Most people die at age 25...

they just don't get buried for another 60 years.

Hello... and congratulations.

Why am I congratulating you? Simple. You're one in a million. By that, I mean you're someone who's decided to take action and take control of your life. Unfortunately, most people just sit on the sidelines, with no plans, no ambitions, and a "whatever" attitude sure to get them nowhere.

But that's not you. You're here... now... reading this book. And that makes you one in a million.

Deciding to read this book is the first and most important step to changing your future for the better. Taking proactive steps toward creating what you want is crucial for your success.

You see, this book you hold in your hands is the key that will help you unlock a different destiny for yourself. By the time you finish reading every word, you will be able to put all the pieces in place and solve the puzzle of success. The mysteries and keys to starting a truly successful life are about to be revealed to you as you read every single page of this book.

WHAT IS SUCCESS?

For the past seven years, I've been on a quest, a journey to understand just what this whole "success" thing is all about. I especially wanted to know why so few students are able to implement the strategies that would enable them to achieve success not just in school but in their lives. I made it my mission to identify the **single most important thing** one would have to learn (then the second and the third and so on because believe me, there isn't just one thing) to become successful.

Now I know you've probably heard many times **success is whatever you decide it to be**. However you personally define it, I believe a majority of people would agree on certain **unifying themes of success.** And in this book, you will learn how to start your journey toward achieving this success.

So I studied people **who started amazing businesses, have great relationships**, **changed the world around them**, and are **admired by their peers**. I didn't limit myself to traditional adult success models, either. I also studied top achieving student leaders, those with high GPAs, and anyone else I felt had managed to achieve and maintain success in life.

Now you may be wondering, "Just what is success exactly?" I won't lie to you. Success is generally measured by results. However, those results can be money, social impact, leadership, and the like. So however you define success, you must always include achievement in the definition.

THE PATH TO SUCCESS

This next concept may surprise you. It certainly surprised me when I experienced it! At first, the **results you will experience will happen inside of you**. You won't see the results of success on the outside, but you will *feel* them. And what you'll learn is that the true journey to success starts with **becoming a success... a winner... at your inner game** before you attempt to succeed in the world around you.

This idea is essential. Most people don't get that, and that's why most people fail. Period. <u>The results first develop internally, then they show up externally</u>.

Now I define success **as living a life you actively create to have the lifestyle you prefer**. That includes living with passion, having freedom, and experiencing the beauty this world has to offer. To put it another way, success is **living a life with no regrets**.

A life with no regrets should not be confused with a life with no boundaries. Living a life of no regrets requires discipline. As motivational speaker Jim Rohn often says, "We must all suffer from one of two pains: **the pain of discipline or the pain of regret**. The difference is discipline weighs ounces, while regret weighs tons." That's precisely what it all comes down to.

Did you know that most lottery winners are broke within five years? MSN Money published an article explaining this phenomenon. It explained that while the winners had a million dollars in the external world, they were internally poor. They hadn't created a foundation within themselves for *lasting* success.

In the book *Secrets of the Millionaire Mind*, T. Harv Eker calls it your "Money Blueprint." People who suddenly become rich will eventually return to their original financial state because being broke is what they know and understand. "Nothing" is the amount of money they can comfortably handle.

YOU ONLY GET WHAT YOU ARE PREPARED FOR

- This concept of having a blueprint applies to all areas of your life, success, and happiness:

- You will not find love if you don't build the capacity within you to have love.

- **You will not have deep friendships** unless you build the capacity within you to have deep friendships.

- **You will never be an A student** if you think you are only capable of a C.

Keep in mind you will only receive what you are capable of receiving. Therefore, your goal must be to **build yourself up** so you can appreciate and handle all of the external rewards you're sure to receive in your life.

Jack Canfield, creator of the *Chicken Soup for the Soul* series, has developed a great analogy for being "ready to receive" in the form of a post office box. If you deliver a package larger than the mailbox it is going to, it won't fit, and therefore it can't be delivered. However, if you deliver a package to a mailbox bigger than the package, it obviously can fit.

Translation: The mailbox is you, and the packages are the things you won't achieve in life if you're too small of a person and unprepared to accept success. The bigger the person you become, the more you can receive from the world.

YOU GET OUT WHAT YOU PUT IN

Let me help you understand the importance of success principles with the following **visualization exercise**.

Imagine you want to go for a drive. No, that's too general for a good visualization exercise. Let's add some details to make this really effective. Imagine you want to go for a drive down the Pacific Coast Highway from San Francisco to L.A. in your dream car, a brand new, candy-apple red Porsche.

You are ready to go, but instead of putting gas in your sporty little ride, you fill 'er up with orange juice. Now I don't care how beautiful that car looks or how amazingly that car drives, **if you don't have the right fuel in the vehicle, you are not going to get very far**. And if you don't fuel your mind with the right knowledge, YOU won't get very far either. You may start out going really fast and looking pretty good, but then the car will eventually break down.

SUCCESS IS A RECIPE

Yes, there is a right way and a wrong way to achieve the life you want. And yes, I will acknowledge exceptions exist to the rule, but let me put it to you like this:

I once heard on the news of this guy who had amnesia. He accidentally got hit in the head with a bat and miraculously regained all of his lost memory after the blow to his head. Just because that worked for him, I didn't see any doctors going around prescribing baseball bats to the back of the head to cure amnesia! So what I'm trying to say is I can't explain why there are exceptions to the rules or why a baseball bat to the head could be a medical miracle, but **I *can* get you started** on your journey to success using principles that have worked for countless people over and over again. I like to call it **"Beginning the Journey."**

WHAT SEPARATES THE TRULY EXTRAORDINARY FROM EVERYONE ELSE IS ONE SIMPLE BELIEF.

"One thought can make you rich,
or it can put you in prison."
-Earl Nightingale

Ideas lead to our beliefs. **And beliefs become part of who we are**.

Do you want to know what the most powerful belief you must have to succeed is? Okay, here it is...

But first, let me tell you about this funny video I saw on YouTube the other day...

Okay, I'm just joking, if this was a text message, this is where I'd type j/k... lol. In all seriousness, the one belief you need to know is

To be successful you must actually
start doing something and then keep going,
no matter what.

With so much information out there right now, what should you read first to get started properly on your journey to success? This book was written to answer that question. It's the starting point for your success. The entire goal of this book is to **get you started and to keep you headed in the right direction**. And you'll be able to do it by following five simple yet powerful principles I call Pillars of Success that will help you develop a solid foundation that will allow you to end up on top in a variety of situations.

WHY THIS BOOK EXISTS

The purpose of this book is to light a fire under you. I don't want you to just read this book and go, "WOW, that was awesome. I feel so great about my future that I'm gonna go lie down, watch a movie, and eat some cookies." Where will that get you?

No. I want you to say, "WOW, this was an amazing book, I can't wait to get started living the life I want, AND I know what I'm going to work on next... right now... today." That's *how* you make things happen.

Unless you know HOW to succeed, you can't. But unless you TRY to succeed, you won't. The five principles discussed in **Your Starting Point** will help you revolutionize your life, without a doubt. But these ideas are not new. The reason I know these principles are sound is because they're **based on the same principles the truly successful have taught for generations**.

BRIDGING THE GAP BETWEEN YOU AND SUCCESS

Right now, a gap exists in your life. A gap exists between where you currently are and where you want to be, between your dreams and your reality. This book will help you close the gap between you and success.

When you finish this book, you will be rejuvenated and totally pumped... ready to take life head-on. But this book is not your life's story; it's just the first chapter—the prologue really. It's a starting, or a turning, point for you.

Look, I don't want to lie to you like a lot of other people out there often do. Many people make absurd comments such as, "This is the only book you will ever need to read," or "This one book has everything you need to succeed." That is a whole bunch of BS. No one book has all of the answers. The bottom line is if you just want to read one book and expect everything to be better, you are crazy.

Think of it like this: if you eat a salad once, will you become healthy? If you just go to the gym once, will you get six-pack abs? Absolutely not! It takes consistent actions over time of choosing healthy foods and working out to get in good shape. Your life is no different, and your success is no different.

BUT... if you get **just one new idea** from this book, then your time was well spent. If you put this book down with at least one concept that shifts your mindset and helps you grow, then you are on the right path. Just one idea could lead to complete success by influencing the decisions you will make from this point on.

HOW TO GET THE MOST OUT OF THIS BOOK

SUCCESS TIP — DON'T JUST READ... LEARN!

My recommendation is to read this book and **choose one of the five principles** to implement into your life. Work on one, then move on to the next, then the next, and then the next. I would also recommend instead of working toward quantity, **work toward quality**. No prize is given to the person who has read the most books and remembered the least. Work on mastery, not just volume.

That is why you should read this book at least twice and use it as a ready reference after you're done. The reason you want to read it twice is that you may miss something the first time, or something may make more sense to you the second time around. The reason why you want to keep referring to it is so you can take a **self-inventory** of how well you are actively applying these principles to your life. You will also have the opportunity to go to **www.yourstartingpointonline.com** to get more resources and materials to help make sure you are moving in the right direction.

I want to save you from making a lot of the same mistakes I've made over the years that countless other people make every single day when they think they are doing themselves a favor by educating themselves through reading. If you have committed this huge mistake before, it's not your fault, because no one told you about it. But now that you are about to discover the solution to this common problem, you have no excuse.

First, allow me to demonstrate by example.

Have you ever sat down to study and read one page of your textbook over and over and over again only to ask yourself "What did I just read? I can't remember anything?!?!" Oh, and it gets better. Have you ever taken an entire class and you can barely remember the name of the teacher who taught it, let alone one thing you learned from the class?!?

Keep it real, has that ever happened to you? Well, what that means is you have what I have diagnosed as "learningus for no reasonus." What you read does not get committed to your memory because it didn't apply to your life, and you didn't take the few extra minutes to find out how it could apply to your life. So here is what you will do differently when reading this book. You will ask yourself and ANSWER the following three questions at the end of each chapter so you can "get" the idea of the principles so you can apply them and use them in your life. Make sense? (PS: It's a good idea to apply this philosophy to everything you are learning, whether in your classes or when you read a magazine, blog post, etc.)

At the end of each section, you will see action steps and questions. Actually go through them to make sure you are learning, not just reading.

CHAPTER II

WHO IS AREL, AND WHY SHOULD I CARE?

Before I can expect you to hear what I have to say, I know you have to first understand why I put this resource together for you. When I got started on my journey to success, I felt like a ton of good information was out there, but nothing that really served as the FIRST book you should read to start you on your journey to a successful life.

The events of my story may differ from yours, but the feeling and the journey may echo similar sentiments. And having insight to where I grew up will shed a lot of light on what drives me now because our **environments play a big role in determining who we will eventually choose to become**.

I grew up on welfare in the projects of Brooklyn, New York, which was a tough neighborhood to say the least. Just to give you a snapshot of the area I grew up in, I grew up across the street from a high school that was named one of the top five worst high schools in New York City. If you know anything about the high schools in NYC, you know that's a really big "accomplishment." It was a tough environment for any kid, and especially rough on a kid like me.

When most people first meet me, they most commonly ask, "So what are you?," as in what ethnicity I am, because I don't seem to fit into any particular category. My dad is a black Jamaican man with Cuban roots. And my mother is a white Jewish woman. Apparently when you put that combination together you get someone who can pass for almost any ethnicity.

I grew up in a predominantly African American neighborhood, and I point that out for a reason. The reason is because growing up in a black neighborhood with a white mother made me very different. It seemed very difficult for people to wrap their brains around the idea that a brown boy (me) was walking around with a white woman (my mom).

As any child quickly learns, whenever you are different, that difference is what people will use against you to pick on you. And I got picked on... a lot. I was called "Oreo" (because I was black on the outside, but white on the inside). There were some other things people called me I can't even mention. It really was a challenge being me. I had no identity.

As an adult, I had a revelation. The things that make us different—the reasons you were made fun of or made to feel weak by others when you were younger—these things can miraculously **become your strengths** as you get older. Sean Stephenson, a fellow professional speaker who was born with a rare disease that makes his bones very brittle and makes him much smaller and different-looking than most people, said all we need to do is change the way we see ourselves, and what makes us different, strange, or weird can become what makes us memorable.

As I grew older, my unique ethnic makeup became a benefit, not a nuisance. It made me unique because I was able to stand out in a crowd. And here's a little secret: **to be successful you have to stand out**. Many successful people you see on TV now were made fun of when they were younger for what makes them famous now. Think about it.

However, growing up, I got picked on a lot for being different and got into a lot of fights as well. Because I constantly felt so different and ostracized, my self-confidence started to tank, and I began hating myself and my environment with an intense, burning passion. My nightmare seemed to really get underway when I saw the first person get shot right in front of my eyes in Brooklyn. Then I witnessed a second person get shot and killed right in front of my building. I have had bullets actually hit my door, been constantly mocked, been robbed at knifepoint, and been beaten up several times. I realized things were getting bad when the sounds of gunshots were no longer a big deal but just background music. All of these events started to make my self-image viciously plummet to nonexistent.

MY SECRET SHAME

For some time, what I am about to share with you was **my biggest, darkest secret**. It is still challenging for me to speak about it, but its subject matter is extremely important, especially if you have ever felt similarly to what I am about to share with you.

I used to live on the sixth floor of my building, and I vividly remember looking out the window down to the ground as well as going onto the roof, looking over ledge, and asking myself, "Should I do it? Is there really anything worth me living for?" I went through many days when I didn't think so. I didn't want to deal with hating myself, others hating me, and feeling like a loser.

I used to fantasize about jumping off the roof and watching people at my funeral crying and missing me, wishing they could have me back because they would finally realize that I was so important to them. I realize now I lacked a feeling of importance and validation, and I thought committing suicide would make me important.

Then I had what Dr. Phil calls one of those "changing moments." My father did something that sparked something inside of me. I think he could sense I was going through some tough times so he decided to take me on a ride in his car to a really nice neighborhood in New York City. As we were driving in my dad's old beat-up car (you know the type, where everything on the car makes noise except the horn!), he pointed to the beautiful houses and cars and said, "One day, you can have that house. Son, you can have that car." At the time, I just looked at him with a blank stare because I didn't see where he was going with it. Having things such as a nice car and a nice home in a nice neighborhood never seemed possible for me.

Why was he saying this to me?

Then he said something I now understand. While it didn't change my life all at once in that single moment, it *did* change me. I carry his words around with me always. He said, "Son, we were given the challenges that we were supposed to be given at birth for a reason—so we can overcome them so that we can become the person we are truly meant to become."

At the time, I didn't get it, but I now understand what he meant. We were all given specific challenges at birth for a reason. They are not problems but tests we are given so we can overcome them to become the best person we can possibly be.

And then I had a thought—a great thought—that maybe it is possible for me to be, do, and have amazing things in my life.

Maybe I could one day overcome my challenges and somehow use them as the vehicle to become something great and help others as well. Maybe I could be the man I saw in my head but didn't think would ever be real. Then after thinking about what he said, I realized **my biggest challenge was hating myself**, my life, and everything around me. If I could figure out how to overcome that, then maybe it would lead me to the life I always wanted. I hoped education would be my way out.

Fast forward to college, where things started going well for me. College was everything I wanted because all of a sudden being smart was cool and helping others was accepted. However, I still fought the internal battle of needing to feel cool. So I made a lot of stupid decisions to "fit in," like drinking and doing drugs to go along with the crowd.

However, I got a rude awakening when I thought I contracted an STD my freshman year but the doctors couldn't figure out what was wrong with me. Weeks went by without any news. During those weeks, I plunged to the lowest point of my life. I thought this was just proof that I didn't deserve to enjoy life, that I was a loser, and that I was destined to be worthless.

Then one day, as I was lying in bed for the seventh day in a row without getting out of it, a voice more pronounced than anything I have ever heard before said to me, "Enough!" That's all I heard, just one word: "Enough." Enough with the self-loathing, enough with the painful thoughts, enough with the victim mentality of "woe is me, my life is so bad," enough with thinking I'm not worthy or a loser. Just plain enough with all of the negativity. I had two options:

I was either going to sink or swim. I was either going to break down or have a breakthrough. It was that simple and that difficult. What was it going to be?

I knew answers to the situation were out there. The only way a problem can even exist is if there is an answer. That is because we live in a world of duality: hot and cold, up and down, and left and right. For something to exist, it must have a counterpart. **So I took a stand** on that spring day and decided that I would swim. No matter what I was about to face, I would persevere. No matter what I went through, I would survive and I would succeed, period. If my life were horrible, then the flip side could be true. My life could be equally as good.

As Napoleon Hill, author of the amazing, life-changing book *Think and Grow Rich!* says: ***"Every adversity, every failure, every heartache carries with it the seed of an equal or greater benefit."*** It seemed I had to hit rock bottom before I could finally pick myself up.

Then I got the phone call that gave me a second chance. The doctors were able to determine what was wrong—it was not an STD—and let me know everything was going to be okay. When I received the good news, I promised myself I would approach life differently. I would enjoy as much as I could and learn all I could about being happy and successful and how to make the right decisions. This was going to be **my starting point for success**.

It has been said the definition of insanity is doing the same thing over and over and expecting a different result. What I was doing in my life wasn't working, and I knew I had to do things differently. At that point, I started the journey of what is now the passion of my life—the trip you are now taking. I call it "**Beginning the Journey.**"

I began searching for a reason to live, a reason to move forward. I became a sponge for knowledge. I began learning from spiritual leaders, reading books on personal development, going to conferences, and listening to audio programs. That year, I found more meaning in my life than the previous eighteen combined. I wasn't sure what I would achieve with this path, but I knew it had to be something better than what I was doing.

As I spent years learning and studying, I found five principles successful people seemed to share, the most important pillars to build a solid foundation for their success structure. These principles helped me start and sell a business, helped me pursue my passion to speak to thousands of students every year across the United States and abroad, allowed me to break the cycle of poverty and get out of the projects for good, and allowed me to live the life I want every single day—all before my twenty-fifth birthday. And these are the five pillars you are about to learn. If you are ready (and I think you are), let's get started creating your success now!

CHAPTER THREE

THE FIRST PILLAR: THE KEY TO CREATING SUCCESS IN YOUR LIFE, FAST

Many people constantly look for the key to success—that mythical secret that once you know it, all of the unknown mysteries of the world will be unlocked, leading to a life of luxury, riches, and happiness. Well, believe it or not, that key actually does exist... to an extent. And you are about to learn it. The only thing I have to tell you is this secret really isn't that much of a secret. And no, it is not some magical mantra you must train with an ancient Tibetan monk for countless years to earn the right to know.

Most people may ***think*** they already know it (the operative word is "think"), but here it is:

"The only person responsible for your life, your results, and your success is you."

The reason why I emphasized the word "think" two sentences ago is because you really don't *know* something until you apply it fully to your life, until you use it consistently and make it part of who you are. Until that point, you have just heard about it, read about it, or spoken about it, but you don't really know it. Knowing comes from application.

Taking responsibility for yourself is the most important, fundamental principle of success you have to "know" to truly become successful. In the classic book *The E-Myth,* author Michael Gerber nails this concept by stating the major difference between extraordinary and ordinary people. Extraordinary people (and I know you want to be extraordinary or else you wouldn't be reading this book) **actively create the lives they want**, while ordinary people passively respond to what has been given to them. Your life begins to dramatically improve when you take responsibility for everything in your life—everything.

▸ PERCEPTION IS REALITY

To properly and actively create the life you want, you have to take full responsibility for your actions and results. All of the successes you have had and the failures you have experienced are all because of you. It is interesting how so many people attribute their success to skill, and their failures to luck or chance. The truth is everything you do or don't do is within your control.

After speaking at a college orientation program about the five pillars discussed in this book, a young lady who was visibly upset approached me. She let me know she had a problem with my presentation. When I asked why, she said everything I said made sense to her except this one principle. I asked her to explain.

She told me a lot of things have happened and still continue to happen in her life that she has no control over. She then told me her chances of success were limited because she grew up poor. She felt if she only had grown up with a rich family who could afford to provide her more things in her life, she would be better and have different results. She wanted to know how could I stand there and tell her she is responsible for growing up poor and not having the same opportunities as others.

At this point, I stopped and took a moment to think about what she had just said, because I could tell she was swelling with emotion and this was a sensitive topic for her. I then replied by saying, "Yes, you are correct. You had nothing to do with where you were born or who your family is. That was out of your control." I visibly noticed her sigh a deep breath of relief, since it seemed as if I were letting her off the hook. Then I said, "Let me ask you a question. Have you ever heard of anyone else who grew up poor, in a bad neighborhood, and with little *opportunity* who became successful?"

She said "Well, yeah, you hear these stories all the time about the American dream, rags to riches stories. What's your point?"

I then said, "Well, do you think any of those rags-to-riches individuals are better than you? Of course they aren't. If another person can do something, so can you. If only one other person came from a similar or worse background than you and succeeded, there is no reason you can't. The only reason you can't is because you tell yourself you can't." Our different backgrounds start all of us out on uneven playing fields, but **the one thing we all have access to is the opportunity for change**. As Henry Ford once said, "Whether you think you can or you can't, you're right!"

You may not be able to change the past, but you can change your future.

You have to just **believe** what you want to achieve and who you want to be are possible. Motivational speaker Les Brown once said you can say two words to yourself that will keep you going when you feel like quitting—if you say and believe these two words, you are on your way to achieve massive success no matter your background. Those two words are "It's possible." When you want something in your life, just say to yourself, "It's possible."

As long as you believe it's possible and you actively move toward your objectives, you will achieve your goals. Taking full responsibility for your life starts with developing a mindset that believes your dreams and aspirations are possible and you will make them come true.

Taking full responsibility for your life means no matter what has happened to you in the past, you are willing to change your future. Taking full responsibility for your life means failure is not an option.

FAILURE DOES NOT EXIST

Most people hate the idea of failing so much they don't do anything worth doing so they won't have to deal with failing. That's crazy! It is perfectly okay to make mistakes—in fact, it is encouraged. As Nobel Prize-winning physicist Frank Wilczek once said, "If you don't make mistakes, then that means you're not working on hard enough problems. And that's a big mistake."

Failure allows you to learn how to become better at a much faster rate. My good friend and successful entrepreneur, Jason Duff, likes to call failure "accelerated learning." It really is true: if you look at failure differently, it will open your mind to different and better possibilities.

Whenever you think you failed at something, change your perspective! Instead of beating yourself up, just think of it as a learning experience. This isn't feel-good psychobabble. It's the truth. Failure is the best teacher out there if you look at it from the proper perspective.

So in truth, every time you fail, consider yourself lucky because you now have the opportunity to learn and grow from that experience. To properly grow from a failure, just ask yourself the following

"What can I learn from this experience?"

Why didn't you succeed? Were you not prepared enough? Did you not take your test seriously? Were you late because you underestimated the traffic? Did you not study enough? Should you not say what you said again? The list goes on and on. And trust me, this "learning from failure" technique **will accelerate your learning curve**, and you will eventually begin to fail a lot less!

GETTING WHAT YOU WANT

In case you didn't know, let me be the first to tell you there is no one who is going to walk up to you and say "Hey, I've been looking for you, I want to give you this six-figure a year job with full benefits, a bunch of vacation time, stock options, company car, and paid-for house. Here you go, have a nice day." The only person responsible for your success is you. If you want a career like that, you have to go out there, find it, and get it.

ADVANCED READING

If you want to find out the little-known way to actually land your dream job, go to **www.yourstartingpointonline.com** to read an exclusive article on how to land your dream job.

THE BIG LIE

A lie has been spread around like a virus and has infected way too many students. The lie is that right now, you are unworthy of actually having or even wanting the things you desire in life. Unfortunately, so many people believe they are not good enough to have that special someone, a nice home, a 4.0 GPA, a college diploma, a nice car, etc.

That idea is a huge, stinking pile of cow poop.

We are all, every single one of us including you, worthy of the best this world has to offer. Why? Because you are alive. Simply because you are living you are worthy of greatness, success, happiness, riches, love, and everything you want. If your heart can feel it, then you're worthy of it. If you weren't worthy, you wouldn't have been born. If you weren't worthy, you wouldn't even have the desire that is the subject of your thought.

Plain and simple, G-d does not make junk. And G-d would not have made you unless there was a purpose for you. So if you have ever felt like you wanted to achieve something but you weren't good enough for it, now you know you are. If you weren't worthy, you wouldn't even have the idea of what you want. Go ahead, think of something you truly would love to have in your life.

Let's say you want to be a dean's list student. Just because you have that desire, you have the right to it. The missing link is that if you want to be an A student but you only see yourself as a C student, you will never break free from the mental image of yourself to take the necessary steps to get those A's. You have to be able to first see yourself as an A student before you can ever become one.

Just because you have the ability to have the thought, you have the right to obtain that goal. It's that simple. You, my friend, are worthy of anything and everything you desire. That dream job, that perfect internship, that great GPA all can be yours with the right mindset that believes you can have these things.

Why? Because once you feel this, you will believe it's possible for you, and that will allow you to start taking the actions an A student would take. Think of what an A student would do (or find out if you don't know) and then do those things.

But here's the caveat: you're entitled to absolutely nothing. I know that sounds harsh, but it's the truth. But consider this...

You're entitled to zilch, zero, nada, nothing... but **you're worthy of everything**. You have to understand the difference. To get what you truly want out of life and school, you are going to have to relinquish your comfy, effortless ride in the passenger side and get into the driver's seat. What this means is kicking excuses out of your life forever. In his book *The True Believer: Thoughts on the Nature of Mass Movements*, Eric Hoffer wrote, "There are many who find a good alibi far more attractive than an achievement."

No one will walk up to you and hand you everything you want. And honestly, if there were someone who could do that, you really wouldn't want that. I'm serious. Believe it or not, the struggle to overcome challenges is what makes accomplishments truly worthwhile. Tom Hanks' character Jimmy Dugan said it best in the movie *A League of Their Own*: **"It's supposed to be hard. If it wasn't hard, everyone would do it. The hard... is what makes it great."**

Think of it like this. Let's say your favorite sport is basketball. Which scenario would you prefer to be in?

- **Scenario 1:** You decide to join one of the most competitive basketball leagues out there. The day before the first game, every other team gets sick and has to forfeit the season, and your team is named the National Champion. You never had to lift a finger, but you are now the champ.

- **Scenario 2:** You decide to join one of the most competitive basketball leagues out there. You play some of the most competitive b-ball of your life. You practice harder than you've ever practiced before; you shed blood, sweat, and tears preparing and playing this season. You barely make it into the playoffs and win each game by less than five points until you advance to the finals. You go all the way to game seven playing one of the best teams in the league. With less than thirty seconds left in the final game of the championship, with your team down by two points, you get passed the ball, shake a defender, get an open shot, and release a three-pointer that lands right as the clock shows "0.00." Now you are the champ!

Which scenario would you rather have happen in your life? The first scenario is completely unfulfilling. The second scenario is what dreams are made of. So even if you could just get handed what you wanted, it wouldn't be as rewarding. In fact, some people say, "Hard work is its own reward."

And the best time to get to work creating your life is right now. I see way too many students just sitting back and waiting for someone to call them up and offer them a dream job, or just sitting back and waiting for Mr./Ms. Right just to walk up to them and introduce themselves. Get real!

Deciding to commit to your success and sticking to it is not always easy. You are going to fail more times than you have ever failed before. Let me just tell you that it is 100% normal. People will say "no" to you over and over and over again... but you only need that one "yes." You only need that one opportunity that changes everything about your life. How you perceive life is your responsibility, and your reaction to the word "no" will greatly influence whether you become extraordinary or remain ordinary.

Think about professional baseball players. A hall-of-fame player will have around a .300 batting average. What that means is that seven out of ten times, the player failed. But the three times he did succeed helped make him a Hall of Famer.

Life works the same way. Countless extremely successful people started out failing more than anyone else. One story I love is that of Sylvester Stallone, the actor who played Rocky. His story is filled with failure after failure of how he became a blockbuster actor. If you want to see the video and hear his amazing journey and how he took control of his life, repeatedly failed, and ultimately succeeded, go to **www.yourstartingpointonline.com**.

When you begin your journey toward success, people will tell you that you are stupid, crazy, and a loser... or worse. People will tell you that you have no idea what you are doing and you won't amount to anything. When you want to find that dream job, tons of companies will say you don't have the proper experience or you are not what they are looking for. Don't worry about the naysayers; they are put here to test your commitment to your goals.

It's normal to experience haters. And when you do, then you know you are doing the right thing! When people start telling you that you can't, in your mind, give them back the t and tell yourself you can.

Look, if you applied for a hundred jobs and got ninety-nine "nos" but got one "yes" that was for your dream job, would you care about the other ninety-nine? Once you realize the power of this and apply it to your life, people will wonder what your secret is, how is it that you are able to obtain so much, and you'll know it's because you understand this principle: you are in control and taking full responsibility for creating the life you want.

‣ MAKING THIS PRINCIPLE REAL

Let's go over a real-world scenario to illustrate taking full responsibility of your life. In this scenario, you are taking a class that is really important for your major. It's a tough class and the professor is extraordinarily mean. You are convinced the professor hates you. You work really hard on the first paper he assigns you, but he gives you a D.

What are you going to do?

A) **Throw your hands up in the air** and say, "It's the professor's fault; there is no way I can pass this class. He hates me, I did a great job on the paper and he still gave me a D. It's not fair! Life sucks."

B) **Stop showing up to class** because what's the point anyway, right? The professor hates you and will fail you no matter what.

C) **Complain to your friends** that you are stupid and that you don't deserve to get your degree and you will drop out of school and work in McDonald's forever!

D) **Realize the paper you wrote did not meet that particular professor's standards.** Schedule a meeting to meet with the professor during office hours to specifically find out what was missing from your paper. Ask yourself why you think the paper could have been better (and actually answer it). Look at how you prepared for the paper and find out how you can better prepare next time. For the next paper, make sure you finish your first draft with plenty of time (at least two weeks) before the deadline to meet with your professor or TA to see if your next paper is up to par. Ask the professor whether you can submit extra credit to help counterbalance the first bad grade you received. Regularly meet with the professor at his office hours to build a relationship with him so you are not just a social security number but a person. And get tutoring at the tutorial center if you find yourself falling behind.

I think you know what the correct choice is. Do you see how this can apply to your life? Can you think of people you know who are not applying this principle to their lives and are suffering because of it? Can you think of times in the past where maybe you blamed others instead of looking inside yourself?

You are responsible for everything. EVERYTHING! How you approach, react, and respond to situations is in your hands.

DON'T GET TOO HARD ON YOURSELF

Often, when people first understand this principle, they initially go through two phases. The first phase is excitement to think about all of the things they can start achieving in their lives. I call that the "honeymoon period." Then they start looking at their current situation and get bummed out because they feel it's their fault they are in the current mess they are in. They shouldn't, because it's **all good news**.

Wherever you currently are in your life is a result of your past actions. Think about it: everything you have in your life is because of what you did in the past. (For example, your current weight has little to do with how much you ate today, but more with all the foods you chose to eat in the past.) If you want to take control of your life for the sake of your future, you have to start today. You have to say you are willing to accept the past and change the future.

What's done is done, but now, today, and for the rest of your life, you will be able to live the life that movies are made of.

▸ JUST BLINK

Now that you have decided to take full responsibility for ALL the things that happen in your life, here's something to notice. No matter how old you currently are, you are going to wish you had begun this journey years ago. You're probably thinking if you had found your starting point years ago, then today you would be where you wanted to be, right? I've got news for you: it doesn't matter how old you are, you would still think that.

If you are eighteen, you would wish you would have started when you were fifteen. If you are twenty-five, you would wish you would have started when you were twenty. If you are forty, you would wish you would have started when you were thirty. If you are eighty, you would wish you would have started when you were seventy. It goes on and on the same way because we all have the "I Need It Now" syndrome.

What do we want? A better life. When do we want it? Now!

The passage of time is not what it seems. I believe in something I call "Just Blink." Time really does go by fast. When you are living it, it goes by slowly, but when you look back, it happened in just the blink of an eye.

Think about this: I bet right now you can remember what your elementary school cafeteria looked like (hopefully you weren't the kid eating the glue!). That was a long time ago, right? But it feels like time just flew by when you think about it. The same thing will happen for your future. Before you know it, it will be five years from today. What life will you be living? Just blink, and you will be in the future.

Let's do a little experiment. Right now, think of an impending deadline coming up in your life. Something not too far away. Let's do your next cell phone payment. That can't be more than one month away. As you read this, "Just Blink," and the next thing you know your cell phone payment will be due. When you get your mind around this concept of time, you'll stop worrying about not having a specific thing now, because if you work properly, you will soon be at your goal.

When your cell phone bill actually *does* come around, I want you to use that as a trigger to say to yourself, "Wow, this Just Blink thing is real. I was just reading Arel's book and now I'm paying my bill." The point of this is to reinforce that even though you probably don't have exactly what you want right now, and it seems like there is a long journey to travel to get to it, literally, **before you know it, you will reach your goal**.

So get excited my friend, the time is now to start creating what you want.

Just for Fun:

> Would you like to have some fun with this? I recommend taking a photo of yourself in a white t-shirt on your birthday every year. This way as the years go on, you can create a flip book to see how you have progressed over the years. (The reason you should wear a white t-shirt is so the clothes will be the same in the picture, and you can just see the progression of your facial characteristics and body type.) It's a lot of fun—try it out.

› AND JUST SO YOU KNOW

It's easy to say "Yeah, I'm in control of my life now," but it's a whole lot harder to actually do it. However, taking responsibility for your life isn't just acknowledging that you are in control. It's also asking yourself **what specific tactics you will use** to implement change.

We'll discuss later in this book other principles to help you take responsibility for your success in life and school. But know that true responsibility is more than words—it's about actions.

‣ LEARNING, NOT JUST READING

To get the most from this chapter, take a moment to do the following Action Steps:

1) Think of a time when you should have taken full responsibility for yourself and didn't. Why didn't you? And how will you make sure to take responsibility in the future?

2) Think of a specific goal you want to achieve now in your life. What can you proactively do right now to attain this goal or move yourself measurably closer to attaining it? Once you figure this out, set a date to actually do it!

3) You are responsible for your results. From now on, resolve to take full responsibility for ALL occurrences in your life, no matter what.

‣ PERSONAL REFLECTION

1) What did I learn from this?

2) How can I apply this principle to my life?

3) What specifically will I do today to apply this principle to my life?

CHAPTER FOUR

THE SECOND PILLAR: THE SECRET TO BUILDING UNSTOPPABLE SELF-CONFIDENCE

This pillar has fundamental importance in all areas of your life. Self-confidence **gives you the edge on the competition** to land you the dream job, find the love of your life, negotiate a better price for a used car, and succeed in school as well as in life.

"People would rather have someone who is strong and wrong than someone who's weak and right."
-Bill Clinton

We gravitate toward people who demonstrate strong self-confidence: we immediately see them as more attractive, more successful, more charismatic, and so forth. But how do you develop self-confidence? What is it? Where does it come from?

Self-confidence is simply defined as the realistic self-belief in one's own judgment, ability, power, and so forth. How can you make sure no matter what happens in your life, your self-confidence is built on an indestructible foundation?

Here's the answer:

The secret to self-confidence is attaching your worth to something that never changes.

This pillar is the true foundation for never losing your belief in your abilities and what you can achieve. In our society, we're taught our self-confidence is based on short-lived things.

We are made to believe we are only as good we look. If you're beautiful, then you should have confidence. If you're smart, popular, athletic, or rich, then you are allowed to have self-confidence. This idea gets perpetuated by celebrities, gossip magazines, music videos, and really everything in the media. And it is the worst bunch of crap I've ever heard.

Nothing can be further from the truth.

At some point, someone will always be smarter than you, better looking than you, faster than you, or stronger than you. When your self-confidence is based on something so trivial as outward appearance, it is extremely easy to shatter it.

The truth is that someone may be better than you at a specific thing, but that doesn't make that person better than you as a person. If you judged how good a lion is based on a dolphin's abilities, the lion would seem pretty inferior. It can't swim as fast, it can't jump in and out of water, and it can't hold its breath for long periods of time.

So then why is the lion the king? A lion judged as a dolphin is inferior, and a dolphin judged as a lion is equally inferior. It's comparing apples to oranges.

I see this all the time when I speak at high schools. A student will come in wearing the newest Nikes and feel like he is the king of the world. "Look at me, I'm good because I have these sneakers." And then somebody comes by with a more exclusive pair plus a hot shirt, jeans, and chain. BAM! The first student's self-confidence goes down the drain. Then it becomes a game you can never win, because you always have to keep up with what's new and hot. In addition to being foolish, it's VERY expensive.

PLANNED OBSOLESCENCE

Have you ever heard of the term "planned obsolescence"? Planned obsolescence is the process of a product becoming obsolete and/or nonfunctional after a predetermined period of time or use. The manufacturer plans or designs this. In other words, all of the things you buy have a predetermined time they will break or go out of style. In fact, fashion and design are set up the same way. You ever notice how companies constantly keep coming out with cooler, newer iPods, computers, and clothing? They do this so if you don't have the newest version of something, you are seen as less cool. The system really is set up to make it next to impossible to stay on top of the latest trends and fashions.

ADVANCED READING

This is a very interesting topic but will go beyond the scope of this book. If you really want to learn more, I recommend you go to www.yourstartingpointonline.com and watch the video "The Story of Stuff" to get the full story on why trying to keep up with the Joneses is foolish at best, and how your stuff is created to make you constantly want to buy new stuff.

WHY SELF-CONFIDENCE IS IMPORTANT

Self-confidence is the cornerstone to great leadership. Bill Clinton's quote at the beginning of this chapter says it best. If you say something with a straight face and confidence, people are more likely to believe you than if you say the same thing in an unsure voice. When I conduct my leadership presentations at colleges, I teach student leaders how to demonstrate self-confidence to their team members so they can get through tough situations by simply acting as they think a confident leader acts.

It's not about lying; it's about **speaking with authority. Let's do a little exercise to illustrate this point**.

- Think of someone you consider extremely successful. Get a very clear picture in your head of this person. Got it? Good.

- Now I want you to think of someone who you think is really unsuccessful or someone you don't want to be like (we all know at least one person like this, keep it real, it's just you and me). Got it?

Okay, now in your mind's eye, get a clear picture of both of them standing side by side. If you had to list out everything you notice about them, what would be one of the first things you notice?

I bet the extremely successful person just exudes a self-assurance the other person does not. To be a leader, which I have a funny feeling you are, having the **self-confidence to lead** is fundamentally important.

▸ THE ONLY THING CONSTANT IS CHANGE

Let me ask you something: have you felt like things are spinning out of control in your life recently? Like there are just about a thousand and one things you need to do in a day, and you don't have enough time to do them all? The next thing you know, the day goes by and you're thinking to yourself, "Damn, I didn't get anything done today!"

You're not alone.

Life is speeding up on you, and change is the only thing that is constant. A lot of people out there are just waiting for things to go back to normal. Let me tell you, they will be waiting for a very long time. Though that feeling of change and having so much to do will never really go away, you can learn to manage it so you are not idling but moving forward.

Often people start to look to others who seem like they have everything in control (key word is "seem") and start comparing themselves to them. If only I could be like Johnny, my life would be better; if only I were as pretty as Tammy, I would be confident. If only I were as talented as Brian, I would have my life in order. Or worse, it becomes I'll never be as good as him or I'm so stupid, I'll never be good at anything.

This self-defeating behavior happens because you're attaching your worth to the outer world, which is inherently transient.

COMPARISON IS STUPID

Comparing yourself to others is a surefire way to sink your confidence through the floor. Studies have shown one of the worst things parents can do to their children is compare them to their siblings. Some of the worst things a parent can say to his child are statements like "Why can't you be more like your brother?" or "Why can't you clean your room like your sister does?"

According to the Public Broadcasting System, this sets up **sibling rivalry** and deflates a child's self-image. It creates a win/lose relationship and causes resentment.

In your life right now, this rule still applies. Comparing yourself to others will **magnify** what you are not good at and cause you to resent both yourself and the person you are comparing yourself to.

Bottom line, don't do it. Yes, it's easier said than done, but you have to work toward it.

It is fine to use other people's talents and accomplishments to motivate you to achieve more, but it is completely unproductive to use what others can do to beat yourself up. As long as you compare yourself to others, you will always find someone better in some area than you are. It's impossible to be the best at everything. So instead of comparing to see what you don't have, recognize **the unique qualities you do have to serve the world** with and work on perfecting those.

In other words, instead of focusing on your weaknesses, **focus on your strengths**. Change your paradigm completely and look at your weaknesses as opportunities for improvement (as much as you looked at "failures" as opportunities for learning.)

This applies to anyone, even celebrities. They probably have it the worst out of all us because the Internet, magazines, and TV scrutinize them based on fleeting characteristics. It's unfortunate, but it's part of the lives they chose. It is a hard life. We hear so many stories of pop stars and actors who cracked under the pressure and suffer from drug use or depression and who sometimes even commit suicide.

I can't even begin to think of all of the headlines Britney Spears has made about the stupidest, smallest things. Britney gains a pound, and the tabloids label her a fat cow. Come on, give me a break. It's ridiculous.

SO WHAT SHOULD I ATTACH MY SELF-WORTH TO?

I had a conversation with a rabbi who worked with Madonna when she was interested in studying Kabbalah. He mentioned something very intriguing. He said Madonna was the perfect example of someone who needed to attach her self-worth to something more than external things. She had everything a person could want: money, fame, good looks, and adoring fans, but she still wasn't happy. What is it she needed? What else should she have attached her self-worth to? She needed to find a deeper level that wouldn't change. For Madonna, her answer was spirituality.

So what should you attach your self-worth to? It's not my place to tell you exactly what that answer is for you. I wish I could say exactly what will work for you, but everyone is different. However, I can tell you what has worked for me and many other successful people in hopes of sparking something within you so you can find what it is for you. For some people, like Madonna, the answer is spirituality. For others, it's religion, science, the Almighty, or one's higher self.

"It" goes by many different names, but It all leads to the same source.

THE MANY FACES OF SPIRITUALITY

This is a good place to make the following statement, as I know it's probably on your mind now. I completely understand the topic of spirituality is a very sensitive subject for many. I am not trying to say one particular way of believing is the proper way. I do believe having a **connection to the Creative Source** is fundamental in building a strong foundation of self-confidence. I have no idea where you currently stand with your spirituality, but we all believe in something...

I once had a friend say it a good way: if you are in a foxhole during war and bombs are exploding overhead, everyone is praying to something! In fact, there's a famous quote that says "there are no atheists in foxholes."

For me personally, I connect my self-worth to G-d (you may notice I spell it without the O, which is just a practice I have out of respect based on my personal religious beliefs). To have a connection to the Creative Source, you don't have to be part of any particular religion, and by all means, I am not saying any particular one is better than another. You just have to find what fits for you.

And I find something very interesting. Whether you believe in science or theology, they both pretty much state the same thing. I first heard this explained by James Arthur Ray in *The Secret*, and I'd like to share it with you.

> If you go to a quantum physicist and ask what created the world, he or she will say "energy." Okay, well describe Energy, It can never be created nor destroyed, always was, always is, and always has been everything that has ever existed has always existed, It's moving in form, out of form, and through form.

Go to a theologian and ask what created the world, and they will say "G-d." Okay, well describe G-d. G-d always was, always has been, can never be created nor destroyed, it's moving in form, out of form, and through form. So if you think you are just some meat suit running around, think again. You are [an] energy field operating in a larger energy field.

So no matter what you believe, the concept that we are part of something greater is universal. The same energy that created the world is within us. If you believe in G-d, then you have the spark of divinity within you and you were created in the likeness of the Creator. If you believe in science, since energy can neither be created nor destroyed, the same energy that created the world is part of you. You have the power of unlimited potential inside of you; it is up to you to unlock that power.

If you believe it to be true, you will now realize that inside of you is something great, inside of you is something unparalleled and amazing, inside of you is potential waiting to be awakened. You are someone extremely important with gifts to be shared with the world. You just have to tap into it, and the first step you must take is believing it is in you.

HOW DOES THIS BELIEF GIVE ME UNSTOPPABLE CONFIDENCE?

So where does the connection between this belief and confidence come from? There are a few steps to really understanding why. Every major belief system will teach some basic similar concepts.

There is a Higher Force at work that created the universe as well as you and me. This Higher Force would not have created you unless you were meant for something great. Our creator wants us to do amazing things.

Think of how a father wants his child to excel, or how proud a parent is at his child's little league game. Our Creator made everything beautiful and would not make junk. Just take a look at nature: nothing exists without a reason. Therefore, just because you are alive, living, and breathing, there is something great that you can and are supposed to do. If you have ever felt as if you were meant for greatness, that is your subconscious mind tapping into the Creative Source letting you know something special is out there for you.

Once you believe this, no matter what happens in your life, you will be good. No one can ever take that connection, that feeling away from you; you'll never lose your confidence. You now know you are connected to the greatest force in the world, and you have a **piece of that power within you**. It's like just finding out you are the child of a king and you are royalty. Can you feel inferior about yourself knowing you are royalty?

▸ EVERYTHING HAPPENS FOR A REASON

I believe everything happens for a reason. Whether good or bad, understood or mysterious, there is a reason. Many times things will happen and you will immediately understand why. Other times, things will happen without a clear reason, but you best believe there is a reason. And that reason will help you become a greater person.

"Every adversity, every failure, every heartache carries with it the seed of an equal or greater benefit."
- Napoleon Hill, author of *Think and Grow Rich!*

Once you truly believe there is something greater for you, that there is a higher force that wants the best for you, you'll see the world through a different lens. You'll know there is nothing that can happen to you and nothing that anyone can say that will stop you from believing in yourself, because you are working on a greater mission in your life. You'll know that what connects you to greatness can only be severed if you allow it to be. You'll know there is **nothing that anybody can do** that can stop you from knowing what you know and who you are.

As long as you have this connection and focus on bettering yourself every day, you will become an unstoppable force.

DEFEATING NEGATIVE THOUGHTS

Even when you develop the strongest belief in yourself, you will still experience negative thoughts. It's normal... and probably the most important personal obstacle to overcome in developing your self-confidence. Negative self-talk is the #1 killer of dreams, ambitions, and goals. It should be on the FBI's Most Wanted list!

Negative self-talk is that voice that says things like "Who are you kidding? You are not good enough," "You're so stupid," "What were you thinking?," and "Everyone hates you." Sound familiar? If it does, you shouldn't feel bad; every single person in the world goes through it.

Successful people learn not to listen to those thoughts. Did you ever stop and think about that? You don't have to believe your own thoughts. You can just tune them out.

This idea was first introduced to me through a book called *The Power of Now: A Guide to Spiritual Enlightenment* by Eckhart Tolle, which is a phenomenal read. If you want to get the true depth of this concept, definitely pick this book up. In a nutshell, what it states is that we don't have to believe our own thoughts. We have multiple levels within ourselves, which you may have heard described as the id, ego, and superego. Basically, we have a negative voice in all of our heads we must fight to control. The negative voice will tell you that you can't, when you know you can.

Most people don't realize this voice is not who we truly are. I know it sounds funky, but it's true. Trying something scary means stepping out of your comfort zone. Back in the day when we were living in the wilderness with wild beasts, this voice probably served some good, warning us, "Don't pet that saber tooth tiger, it's not your friend!"

But today, that voice doesn't serve us anymore. When that voice speaks up, just acknowledge it and recognize it's not coming from your true self. T. Harv Eker says it best in *Secrets of the Millionaire Mind*: just tell that voice, "Thank you for sharing," cancel it, and push it out of your head like a cloud floating away. Those negative thoughts are not really part of who you are. Soon you'll realize you can overcome them. The negative thoughts never really go away: successful students and leaders just know how to control them and minimize their impact. Your confidence will grow as you learn to pay less attention to that overly negative voice and focus on the voice inside of you that says you can achieve your goals.

It's a long process, but a process worth investing in.

RUNNING & READING

Actor Will Smith put it best in a powerful acceptance speech he once gave after winning a Kids' Choice Award in 2005. He said the key to defeating self-negativity is running and reading. Running? Where does running fit into overcoming negativity?

When you are running, a negative voice tells you that you can't do it, that you are not good enough, that you should stop before you really reach your goal, that you should not stretch yourself, and that you shouldn't keep running because your lungs are about to pop. Once you learn to overcome that negative voice you'll learn not to quit when life gets hard. Running will help you **train your mind to ignore that voice**. You not only practice a great discipline of self-growth, but you also get yourself into the best shape of your life, which will boost your self-confidence. I don't know about you, but when I look good, I feel good too.

Why reading? There is no problem you can face that someone else hasn't already faced, overcame, and wrote a book about. ***Your Starting Point for Student Success*** is just such a book.

The key is to constantly keep putting good stuff in your mind and programming yourself for success. Success is not a one-time event; it is a continual process that takes time and dedication. Many times if we just knew how to overcome our challenges, we would. Books are the keys to all the answers you seek. There is an unfortunate joke that says if you want to hide something valuable from young people, put it in a book. You constantly need to keep striving to read, learn, and apply what you've learned to your life. Lack of confidence usually stems from not knowing what will happen next. The more you read, the more you will know how to handle situations, which will make your confidence soar.

If you would like to see the full video of "Running and Reading", just go to **www.yourstartingpointonline.com**.

YOU ARE A KING OR QUEEN RIGHT NOW

Let me paint a picture for you. Let's say you have been living your life the way you have already been living it. Then one day, you get a letter in the mail and you find out you are the heir to the throne of a faraway land. You now have abundant riches, power, potential, and honor. Let me ask you a question. If at the same time you found this out, someone was making fun of the shoes you were wearing, would you really care? Of course not: it wouldn't mean anything to you because you are royalty!

That is exactly what you have just found out. You are royalty. You are a child of G-d, the predecessor you are the heir to is the King of the world. Not bad huh? So when someone tries to make you feel like you are less than you know you are, just remember who you are and whose you are. As royalty, no peasant should ever make you feel down about the amazing person you are.

This is my belief. What is yours going to be? You have the ability to believe whatever you wish. It's been said the only thing we have 100% control over in this world is what we think. I agree.

You can either think you are tied to greatness or not. What will you choose?

Remember: as long as you are breathing, this means you have the potential to do something great. Once you find you truly understand this, hold onto that feeling. I encourage you to go on a journey to find what you can connect your self-worth to and what will work for you. It doesn't have to be what other people tell you it's supposed to be, but it has to be something greater than you. Once you know it and feel it, nothing will prevent you from moving forward with 100% unstoppable self-confidence.

▸ LEARNING, NOT JUST READING

To get the most from this chapter, take a moment to do the following Action Steps:

1) Spend ten minutes reflecting on what you will choose to connect your self-worth to. What is something in your life you feel connected to but need to develop more deeply?

2) To debug the negative thoughts in your head, you have to reprogram them with positive thoughts. Go into a room where you can be by yourself, look in the mirror right into your eyes, and say five times out loud, "I am strong, I am confident, and I am good looking!" (Have some fun with this, and say it like you mean it!) Repeat this step daily for one month. Trust me, starting your day like this will make you feel like a million bucks!

3) Make a list of your unique talents and strengths. Look at them with pride and figure out what you want to focus on developing more deeply.

4) Make a list of at least ten accomplishments you are proud of (you can do this, just spend some time thinking about awards you've won or things you were proud to do).

PERSONAL REFLECTION

1) What did I learn from this?

2) How can I apply this principle to my life?

3) What specifically will I do today to apply this principle to my life?

CHAPTER FIVE

THE THIRD PILLAR: THE MISSING INGREDIENT AND HOW TO GET MORE DONE IN LESS TIME

Now that you've learned the keys and little-known secrets to taking charge of your life and are developing amazing self-confidence, what will you do with it? That is what our Third Pillar is all about. The Third Pillar is quintessential to your success because it deals with the one concept that will put all the principles you learn into play. The Third Pillar deals with the one thing most people just don't do, and if you don't, you'll never be a successful student. It's the one thing that separates the Haves from the Have-Nots. If you don't do this one thing, all the knowledge in the world means absolutely nothing.

You've probably heard that knowledge is power, right? WRONG! Knowledge is only **potential power**. It's **what you do with that knowledge** that is powerful. So what is this one thing?

You must take action—not just action, but consistent action!

Simple, but true. Successful individuals are well-known for taking action on a consistent basis toward their goals and not quitting until they reach their destination.

Most people are really good at talking about what they want to do, but very few people are good at actually doing it. My father always told me I should not be part of the "Gunna" family. Have you heard of the Gunna family before? This is the group of people who say, "You know what, tomorrow I'm gunna do this and I'm gunna do that." In the end, "all talk and no action" does not produce results. If you find yourself saying, "I should do this, and I should do that," all that happens is you end up doing nothing but "should-ing" all over yourself!

A subset of this family is the Shoulda-Woulda-Coulda people. They should have done something, but now it's too late. They would have done something, but the circumstances weren't perfect. They could have done something, but they didn't.

You can imagine how far in life the Shoulda-Would-Couldas and the Gunnas will get.

One of the main differences between successful people, like you and me, and everyone else is successful people take action toward their goals as a **daily** habit. If you want to know how to get more done in the next thirty days than you have in the last five years, whether it's organizing your class and social time or organizing your studying, this is the technique to implement. Our Third Pillar is called "3 to Succeed," which in a nutshell means:

Take three specific, measurable, actionable steps toward your goals every single day.

ARE YOU A C PERSON OR AN O PERSON?

Many students right now are good at starting things but horrible at finishing. I call them "C people." A select group of students are out there accomplishing their goals in life; I call them "O people." C people are those who start many projects but don't finish any of them. They have all of these half-open circles that need to be completed and transformed from a C to an O. As long as they don't complete the projects they start, their lives are always going to be filled with stress and unhappiness because they will have no sense of accomplishment. The O people start on a goal and then complete it.

What type of person will you commit to being?

LESS IS MORE

Taking action toward your goals in school and in life every single day will be the difference between actually creating the life you want and just dreaming about it. The problem most people face is they stop taking action before they achieve their goals, or they quit soon after starting because they've lost the motivation to continue.

It happens every year, all over the country, right around January 1st.

Does the term New Year's Resolution ring a bell? I once heard top-selling author and motivational speaker Tony Robbins break it down perfectly. He mentions how people say to themselves that every single morning, they are "gunna" wake up at 5 am and run three miles.

So here's what happens. The first morning, they get up, jump out of bed at 5 am, and run like they are training for the Olympics! They start telling everybody they see about their "accomplishment" that they are making things different in their lives and they are in the "habit" of running three miles every morning while everyone else is still sleeping.

Sooner than later, the **excuse monster** starts rearing its ugly little head. "Man, it's a little cold outside, I didn't get enough sleep last night, and plenty of sleep is part of a good health regimen, isn't it?, I don't want to push myself too hard, let me just get a few more minutes of sleep." Then you start *rationalizing* that tomorrow will be different, and when tomorrow becomes today, the task gets put off until tomorrow again. People start rationalizing all the reasons why they can't do whatever it is they promised to do.

The funny thing about the word "rationalize" is when you break it down into its syllables, it sounds like the words "ration-lies." What most people are doing when they rationalize is just "rationing lies" to themselves about all of the reasons they aren't accomplishing the goals they want for themselves. This process can be avoided. Most people try to do huge things all at once and fail. Most people try to run before they learn to crawl, and that is a recipe for guaranteed failure.

It's **better to take small baby steps** to make consistent change. Less really is more.

THE SECRET OF THE SLIGHT EDGE PHILOSOPHY

3 to Succeed is about **doing small things consistently over time to reach your goals**. If you want to be successful in school and in life, then you cannot be in the habit of doing a lot of things at once and then sitting down, resting on your laurels, and hoping everything will work itself out. Instead, you should use the slight edge.

So here's what the slight edge says: it's the little things we do every single day, consistently, over time that compound into massive results.

Jeff Olson, author of *The Slight Edge*, puts it a great way:

> If you were to improve just .003 each day—that's only 3/10 of one percent, a very Slight Edge—and you kept that up for the next five years, here's what would happen to you:
>
> The first year, you would improve 100 percent (you would already be twice what you are today). The second year, you would improve 200 percent. The third year, 400 percent. And the fourth year, 800 percent. And by the end of year five—by simply improving 3/10 of one percent each day—you will have magnified your value, your skills, and the results you accomplished 1,600 percent. That's 22 times more than you are today.

It's amazing when you look at what little effort compounded over time will yield. In fact, when asked to name the greatest invention in human history, Albert Einstein simply replied, "compound interest." Compound interest makes people rich.

Compounded action makes people successful.

Tell me whether this scenario sounds familiar to you. Let's say you have an exam coming up. You study really hard for the test and stay up all night cramming the information into your head. You take the test. What happens over the next few days? You forget almost everything, right? Or the experience of studying so hard is so draining you don't even want to think about picking up a book for at least another two weeks, which turns into three weeks, which turns into a vicious cycle of constantly pulling all-nighters before your exams.

The truth is we don't ever have to do all-nighters. Your exams are never a surprise, are they? You always know exactly when your finals and midterms are. There's this little thing called a syllabus. I've never heard of a professor giving a pop final. So rather than cramming in a brutal all-nighter, you can review your course work each day and **compound** the effects of your studies.

The bottom line is little steps done over time produce the best and least stressful results.

"Little hinges swing big doors."
-W. Clement Stone

DOING SMALL THINGS OVER TIME TURNS INTO BIG RESULTS

You are in a marathon, not a sprint. I know, I know. It's hard to think of waiting X number of months to attain a goal you want right now. But remember the Just Blink philosophy from Chapter 3? **You have to focus on the little things you can do** now that will pay massive dividends in time. We've all heard it's the little things that count. Jeff Olson describes it this way:

> The slight edge is easy to do—and it is easy not to do. Now, I'm defining EASY here as simply "something you can do." The Slight Edge philosophy is based on doing things that are easy—little disciplines, which, done consistently over time, add up to the biggest accomplishments. The problem is that all those things that are easy to do are just as easy not to do. Why is something easy not to do? Because if you don't do it, it won't kill you today. But, that simple, seemingly insignificant error in judgment, compounded over time, will kill you, destroy you, ruin your chances for success, and demolish your dreams. You can count on it."

Let's make this theory practical. If you drank one glass of water, would that make you healthy? Absolutely not. If you went to the gym only once, would you get six-pack abs? No way. However, working out consistently and drinking water daily will absolutely change your health and your body for the better.

Here's an example of how you can apply the slight edge to improving your health.

Wake up every single morning and immediately do ten push-ups and drink one glass of water, that's it. If you can't do ten push-ups, do five. If you can't do five, do three. As soon as you wake up, open your eyes and jump on the floor, do 1, 2, 3, 4, 5, 6, 7, 8, 9, 10 and chug a glass of water. At most, this will take forty seconds of your time. You won't even think anything of it. What will happen is this will become part of who you are, part of your routine. This one act done consistently will eventually lead to better choices.

From this one simple act, your health over time will dramatically improve. Why? Because one day, effortlessly, you're going to say to yourself, "You know, ten just is not working for me anymore, I'm going to do fifteen push-ups instead." Then you're going to want to go to the gym or an exercise class or join a sports team. One glass of water turns into two, into three, and so on and so forth. Good eating choices start to replace bad. And to be a successful student, you MUST take care of your health.

One simple choice can change everything. But by the same *token*, not making one simple choice can change everything as well... and not for the better! Not doing anything for your health is definitely going to have negative effects over time.

Let's say your professor assigns you a twenty-page paper to write and gives you a deadline thirty days away. By just writing one page a day, you can have your paper done in time to get it reviewed by your professor, write a second draft, and still have time to party with your friends... stress-free!

▸ THE INGREDIENTS OF THE 3 TO SUCCEED RECIPE

To achieve more in the next few weeks of your life than ever before, just focus on doing three main things every single day that will move you at least a little bit toward your goals. It's simple, but most people have no idea how to properly set goals and, most importantly, how to achieve them in a day.

So starting today, every day, I want you to **set three SMART goals** you can accomplish before you go to sleep at night. The word SMART is actually a mnemonic memory device to help you remember how to properly focus your goal setting. SMART stands for:

S—Specific

M—Measurable

A—Action-Oriented

R—Reachable

T—Time-Sensitive

One of the biggest mistakes people make when setting goals is not following the above formula. Most **people's goals are so vague** they have no idea what they should be doing... or when they've actually accomplished their goals! Let me give you an example...

How many people do you know who have set the goal to make more money? (Maybe you're one of those people.) It's a perfectly fine goal, but here's the problem: if your goal is just to "make more money," what does that mean? If I give you one more penny than you previously had, isn't it true you made more money? That really isn't what you would want, is it? One more penny isn't going to negatively or positively affect your life in any way.

You have to be crystal clear on what you want to achieve. Be specific. Words like "more," "better," and "soon" don't have any meaning. You don't want to make "more" money; you want to increase your monthly income by $250. You don't just want a better GPA; you want at least a 3.5. Make sense?

▸ CASE STUDY WITH SMART GOALS

The concept of SMART goals may be a little challenging, so let's apply the SMART goal-setting formula to the vague "make more money" goal. This goal will now become:

Within 24 hours of earning any money,
I will put 10% of everything I make (paychecks, gifts, etc.) into my online savings account.

Now let's hold it up to the **SMART rubric** to see how well it holds up.

- **Is it Specific?** Yes, I know the way I will make more money is by saving more of the money I already have.

- **Is it Measurable?** Yes, I can measure 10% of the total amount of money I receive.

- **Is it Action-Oriented?** Yes, I have to actually do something once I get the money.
- **Is it Reachable?** Yes, I am working within the money I already make, so there is no problem there.
- **Is it Time-Sensitive?** Yes, I know within twenty-four hours of receiving money, it will go into an online savings account.

A "yes" answer to all these questions means you're being SMART in your goal setting. And now that you have a clear goal in mind (saving 10% of your money), you also have to set up **mini-goals** to help you eventually achieve your main objective.

Some of the mini-goals for the above example would include:

<u>Day 1</u>

1. Research three different online savings accounts by the end of the day.
2. Spend no more than two hours researching through Google the most important aspects in choosing the proper online savings account.
3. Spend at least thirty minutes comparing the benefits of the different online savings accounts (interest rate paid, ease of use).

Day 2

1. Choose the online savings account I will open before end of the day.

2. Register my information with the online savings account I chose before Monday.

3. Before my next paycheck, set up direct deposit with my job so my paycheck gets directly deposited into my bank account (bye-bye paper checks).

Day 3

1. Call my bank and online savings account provider to find out how to automatically get 10% of my paycheck automatically deposited into my online savings account.

2. Go through the steps the bank explained to me to set up the automatic transfer of 10% of all money that goes into my checking account.

3. Check my bank account when my first direct deposit happens to make sure everything was set up properly.

ADVANCED SAVINGS

By the way, if you haven't already done this for yourself, I recommend doing it ASAP. Go to **www.yourstartingpointonline.com** to get a list of online savings accounts that offer the best rates.

THE FOUR WORDS THAT WILL ALWAYS MOTIVATE YOU

You can attach four words to your goals that will help keep you motivated toward achieving them. Those four words are:

"So That I Can."

The "So That I Can" is the most important part of your goal because what comes after it is **what really motivates you**. Going to the gym isn't exciting, but going to the gym "so that I can" look great in a bathing suit this summer IS exciting... and motivating.

Let's say your goal for the semester is to get on the dean's list. For that to happen, you need at least a 3.5 this semester. So the goal of merely getting a 3.5 transforms into the goal of getting a 3.5 this semester **so that I can** get into a top med school. This technique will allow you to focus on the benefit you'll get from accomplishing that specific goal.

A lot of students write "4.0" on an index card, tape it to their desks, and look at the number 4.0, but there's no feeling behind it. It's just a number. The "So That I Can" gives you the emotion needed to take massive action. And without a good enough reason, most things seem to find a way of not getting done.

TAKING ACTION WITH 3 TO SUCCEED

Here's how you can start using 3 to Succeed today to start skyrocketing toward your success.

First you will need a **pack of index cards**; you can get them from the dollar store. Write your main goal down on the back of the index card on the blank side. Let's imagine your dream is to become a doctor one day, so that you can help keep children healthy. You would write the following on the back of the card:

I will have a 3.5 this semester, so that I can get into a top med school.

Starting today, (yes, today, I don't care what time it is) you will set three specific goals you want to accomplish for the day.

You will **set at least two academic goals and one life goal daily.** Setting an academic goal is pretty self-explanatory; it's a goal that moves you toward academic success. But there is much more to success as a student than just what you do inside the classroom, so the life goal will cover the outside of the classroom stuff.

For example, if you wanted to become a doctor, your goals could look like this:

<u>Academic</u>

1. I will read three chapters of my biology book today before 5 pm.

2. I will attend the chemistry study group tonight at 8 pm.

<u>Life</u>

3. I will call three doctors' offices today before noon to see if at least one of the doctors would be interested in being interviewed by me so that I can find out how the doctor chose his or her particular specialty.

That's the recipe. Two academic, one life. Now I know what you are probably thinking: "Arel, there are WAY more than three things I need to do in a day!" And I understand that. You live a busy, active, exciting life. **But under no circumstances do these three things not get done**. They are nonnegotiable.

Many times in the day we get inundated with so many things to do that the most important stuff gets put on the back burner of your To Do List. Not this time! The 3 to Succeed goals you write on this particular list should get done as soon as you possibly can.

Oh, by the way, you do have an actual, **physical To Do List**, right? Not just something you keep in your head, but something you can look at. A huge mistake many people make is trying to keep something in their heads, because they are guaranteed to forget something. As the ancient Chinese proverb says,

The faintest ink is better than the best memory.

Case in point, have you ever gone to the supermarket to buy eggs and come home with bags full of groceries, but no eggs? Be honest. Using **lists is a critical tool of the successful**.

Now that we've settled that argument, I want you to write down your big goal with a "so that I can" on one side of the card, and your 3 to Succeed action steps on the other. The following is how it might look:

I will get a 3.5 GPA this semester so that I can set myself up to land my dream job

- I will research 5 sources today for my History 104a Paper
- I will read 3 chapters in my Psychology 111 textbook
- I will call three potential mentors today to set up a time to interview them about their story

THE "SECRET 8" TRICKS TO GETTING MORE DONE IN LESS TIME

There are way too many C people out there and not enough O people. I want you to be an O person.

Many C people genuinely care about their goals and are not lazy. Any C person can become an O person by learning the special formula you are about to learn.

SECRET #1: KNOW YOUR VERY NEXT STEP

Knowing specifically what your next steps are will keep you constantly moving forward. A huge stopping point for many students is having no clear idea what to do next. Here's something to think about: **when we don't know what to do next, we do nothing**.

Let me know if this scenario sounds familiar. John is your classic C person. He has a paper to write. John sets a vague goal of "getting my paper done." However, it is unclear what his very next *actionable* step will be. So John will sit down, stare at his computer screen, move papers around on his desk, and right before he starts, he will check his Facebook account, see a newsfeed of someone's new photo album, and check it out.

Then all of a sudden, five hours of his life have disappeared and he has accomplished nothing with his paper. Sound familiar?

Let's change his goal from vague to specific: "I will complete my paper by Friday of this week so that I can enjoy my weekend stress-free." An actionable step to help him get started is "I will go to the library after my English class and ask the librarian to help me find three books and then use Google to find two Internet sources."

With this action step, he knows exactly what he has to do, where to go, and whom to ask for help.

What this also means is there will be planning involved. Most people don't like planning, but as Brian Tracy states in his book *Time Power*,

"Every minute in planning saves you ten minutes in execution."

So six minutes of planning will save you one hour of time. Not bad, huh?

SECRET #2: SET A DEADLINE

We all work on deadlines. Without deadlines, nothing would get done because "tomorrow" always seems be the best day to start something you really aren't too excited about. Setting a deadline creates **a sense of urgency to complete your goal**.

A deadline puts a healthy pressure on you to start taking action. Start using the power of deadlines in everything in your life such as finishing your résumé, writing a handwritten letter to a loved one, and buying your first car. Literally everything you want to achieve must have a deadline.

The only difference between a dream and a goal is a deadline.

Let me give you an example of the power of deadlines. Let's say on February 1st you get assigned a fifteen-page paper due March 25th. What day is that paper getting done? Keep it real, March 24th (and for some of us, March 25th really early in the morning, right?).

The deadline is what makes you take action.

What is interesting is that many students seem to only need one day to write an entire paper. So perhaps we should only be given two days to write our papers. (Just kidding—that would not be fun AT ALL!)

One of the worst things you can do to **sabotage your success** is wait to get something done "when you feel like it" because chances are you will never feel like it. In school, we have deadlines for papers and dates for exams, but **in life there is no authority figure to set a deadline** on the things you need to accomplish to become successful.

You have to be that authority figure in your own life. (Remember the First Pillar? Take responsibility!)

SECRET #3: USE REVERSE ENGINEERING

As we already talked about in the SMART goals section, mini-deadlines are the underused tool that will make you a champion. Mini-deadlines are your secret weapon to finishing projects on time. But how do you properly set mini-deadlines?

USE REVERSE ENGINEERING.

Reverse engineering simply means that you:

- **Start with the end in mind.**
- **Work backwards** from the finished result to where you are today, figuring out what needs to be done to get to that end goal.
- **Set mini-deadlines** between now and then to get all of the tasks done before the final deadline.

So if your paper is due on the 25th, you want to set up a deadline to finish your first draft and a deadline for someone to review it.

At first, you might not know what to do. A good technique is to **observe yourself** as you go through the process of writing a paper, making notes of the steps you are taking as you are doing them. You will have to make yourself aware of each step you are taking and **write them down**. This list will serve as your **"Paper Writing System"** or manual for all of the papers you will write in the future.

So your Paper Writing System might look like:

1. Type the name of my possible subject into Google to see what other people have written about it.

2. Brainstorm ideas for topics I could write about based on the samples I read.

3. Come up with a list of at least three potential ideas I would like to talk about in my paper.

4. Turn possible paper topics into questions.

5. Answer those questions to develop my thesis statement. Etc. etc. etc.

* Just a side note: **creating systems** is what all successful people do for most aspects of their lives. Even when people don't work, systems do. When you jot down the steps you take to write a paper, you will **never have to worry again** about not knowing what your next steps are because you'll already have them written down. This little bit of planning will save you tons of time in the future. And if you don't know how to create a system to write a good paper, you should ask someone who gets good grades, your TA, or a tutor how they do it.

SECRET #4: KNOW WHAT YOU WANT

Do you know the number one reason why people don't get what they want out of life? They don't know what they want. A lot of people say things like "I just want to be happy," but they've never defined what makes them happy. Knowing what you want is going one step further than most people will. Most people will stop at "I want to be happy," but that's vague and nonspecific.

If you want to become happy, you must take it one step further and decide what makes you happy: more money, more free time, less stress, a bigger house, a pony, it doesn't matter what it is... It seems simple, but it's true: if you can't specifically see what your goal is you will never reach it.

To be honest, most people don't know what they want, but they *do* know what they don't want. I see it over and over again. When I speak at college orientations or career weeks, a lot of students tell me they don't want a job that sucks after graduation, but they have no idea what they want to do. Understanding that, I created a presentation called **"Turning Your Passion into Your Profession."** Students who attend this event leave knowing exactly what they must do to love what they do as a profession and most importantly how to land that dream job!

During that presentation, we have everybody write down the things they don't want in a job. Then we sort this list into two categories: "Never Acceptable" and "Could Live With It." Then I ask them to state the positive version of each negative job attribute. It's a great strategy for figuring out what you want.

For example:

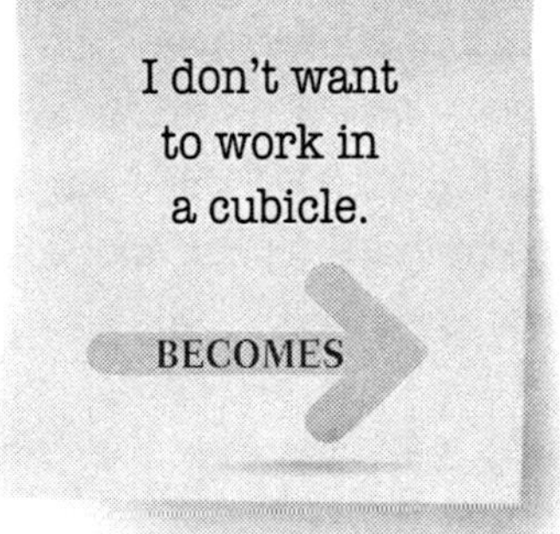

I want a work
environment
that allows
me the freedom
to travel.

‣ SECRET #5: KNOW WHY YOU WANT IT

Understanding why you want something is the key to staying motivated. Understanding the "Why" is a very crucial step many often overlook. The "Why" is what will drive you when you want to quit.

Have you ever started something, been really excited about it for a little while, and then just suddenly stopped doing it? Like anything in life, the honeymoon phase of most activities makes you feel like you are on cloud nine. For example, when you first start dating someone, he or she may seem perfect, or when you first start a class, the subject matter might seem so interesting. Then when that first phase wears off, most students just throw in the towel on relationships, on learning, on getting in shape, or whatever it is they really want.

The reason this happens is because they are not holding onto **why it is important to them**.

The quest to get a 4.0 is always an exciting one during the first week of classes. Staring into the mirror after the first few classes, student members of the Gunna family across the country say, "You know what, this semester is gunna be the semester I'm gunna get straight As!" And then after a few weeks when the real work starts, the determination it takes to get that 4.0 drops to the point they'd much rather stick a pencil in their eyes then open their textbooks.

To overcome this, you must know why you want that 4.0. What is it about getting a 4.0 that will make you really excited? Not just normal excited, but vibrating off the walls excited! Is it being able to make your parents proud? Is it because you need to maintain a certain GPA to keep a scholarship or to get into the grad school of your dreams, which will let you get that dream job you've so badly wanted?

Your "why" has to be bigger than any adversity you will face. If the only reason you want a 4.0 is because it would be cool, that's not going to cut it as a motivational tool. However, if getting a 4.0 would mean you would receive $1,000,000, I bet you would be busting your hump all semester, am I right? Nothing would stand in your way of that 4.0 if you knew that kind of cash were on the line.

Trust me, you can get a 4.0 if you are dedicated. You just need to make sure why you want it is more important than any excuse you can rationalize to yourself. Got it?

▸ SECRET #6: DO THE TOUGHEST THINGS FIRST

"Eat a live frog first thing every morning and it's doubtful anything worse will happen to you all day."
- Mark Twain

To be more productive with goals you set, tackle the toughest parts of your tasks first. Normally, the toughest part is **the part that causes the most stress** and is probably the reason why most students won't finish a project and remain a C instead of an O person.

Where most people go wrong is they do all the little and easy things first to get them out of the way so they can focus on the major task of the day. Usually what happens is all those little (usually less significant) things eat up your time, and then you eventually decide to put your large/important task off until the infamous "tomorrow." Then this cycle repeats itself over and over until it messes you up completely and you get completely stressed out!

To avoid this, **start with the toughest part first when your energy level is at its highest**. If you can't figure out what is the most important thing for you to do, the best technique to identify it is figuring out which part you are procrastinating on doing the most. My good friend Michael Simmons, author of *The Student Success Manifesto*, taught me that usually

The thing we procrastinate on the most or have the most resistance to wanting to do is most likely the most important next step.

Once you identify what that particular task is, focus on the benefit you will gain from completing the task, not the actual arduousness of the task itself. Then suck it up and start working on it ASAP.

The stress in your life will dramatically drop when you take this approach to school and to life. Usually the anticipation of the work is much worse than the actual work itself. If you want to call a company to get an internship or job, the anticipation of making the phone call is much worse than the actual phone call itself. The more you apply this principle, the more you will truly understand it.

SECRET #7: ASK THE EXPERTS

At almost every campus I visit or student leadership retreat I speak at, a student usually asks me this question: "But Arel, what if I know what I want to do but I have no idea how to do it?" My answer is usually one and the same:

Find someone who has done what you want to do and ask that person how you can do it too.

If you want to climb Mount Everest, you could go it alone (not recommended), or you could get an experienced guide who has climbed to the mountaintop plenty of times before who can show you how to do it.

As a student, you have access to so many resources that people outside of school have to pay a pretty penny to access. Your professors are some of your most important resources. As a student, you can go to office hours and get help on various subjects. In the real world, that kind of help is called "consulting" and could cost up to a couple thousand dollars an hour. But as a student, all the million-dollar guidance is yours... FREE. Don't underutilize your resources, especially for your actual schoolwork.

ADVANCED LEARNING

Go to **www.yourstartingpointonline.com** to find out how to dramatically improve your GPA by just asking your professor one simple question.

You'll be surprised who will help you simply if you ask for help. All you have to say is "Hi (person's name), my name is (your name) and I would love to learn how to do X better, I was wondering if you wouldn't mind helping me figure out how to do it?"

Think about it: experts are people who have already made all of the mistakes and can show you the quickest way to succeed in a field. Why try getting through a wall by banging your head against it, when you can ask someone on the other side where the door is and how to find it? And if you can't get face-to-face access to the experts you need, try another expert, www.google.com. You'd be amazed what questions you can type in and get answered through articles and websites.

A problem cannot exist without a solution. Do yourself a favor and seek the answer from someone who knows instead of trying to do everything yourself. If you need help finding a job, ask a professor if he or she has any connections. Need help managing a project for a school organization? Ask a management professor. Need help working out your budget? Ask a finance professor. The list goes on and on. All you have to do is ask for help.

Do you want to know how to easily get more out of life? **Just ask for what you want and ask for help when you need it.** You'll be surprised how this little technique will bring so much into your life.

SECRET #8: AVOID ANALYSIS PARALYSIS

Analysis paralysis is a huge mistake many students make that stops them from achieving what they want. Analysis Paralysis happens when people spend so much time waiting for the perfect time to do something they never actually do it! There is always something else to research or something you're not 100% comfortable with yet. No matter how much planning and research we do on anything, we will never know everything about it—that's literally impossible.

Don't get me wrong—research and planning is crucial for your preparation to success, **but taking action is what will actually make you successful**.

You can read every book on how to swing a baseball bat, watch every baseball game, study videotapes of a home run hitter's swing broken down frame-by-frame, and it won't mean anything until you actually get up to the plate and swing at a few pitches. The late business guru David Sandler really summed it up with one of his book titles: *You Can't Teach a Kid to Ride a Bike at a Seminar.* One step in the right direction is more valuable than years of thinking about it. This means if you want to be a leader, you need actual experience leading. No matter how much preparation you do, you won't be good at it until you actually do it.

So whatever it is you want, ready or not (the truth is we never truly feel ready), go after it. You'll learn a lot more from doing, failing, and regrouping than from just thinking about it.

PUTTING IT ALL TOGETHER

So here is how you will set and reach more goals than ever before:

- First, know what you want. What is the goal you want to achieve?
- Set a deadline.
- Know why you want the goal and what the motivation behind achieving this goal is.
- Use reverse engineering to start at the end goal and work your way back to where you are today, setting up mini-deadlines to achieve the goal.
- Determine what the toughest part about your project is and tackle that first before anything else.

- If you find yourself not knowing what or how to do something, seek the advice of people who know what they are doing and ask for help.
- Know that the conditions do not have to be perfect before you start.
- And then actually do the work!

LEARNING, NOT JUST READING

To get the most from this chapter, take a moment to do the following Action Steps:

1) Buy a stack of index cards.
2) Write down a goal with a "So That I Can" for this month, this semester, and this year.
3) Choose your month's goal and reverse engineer how you will obtain it.

PERSONAL REFLECTION

1) What did I learn from this?
2) How can I apply this principle to my life?
3) What specifically will I do today to apply this principle to my life?

CHAPTER SIX

THE FOURTH PILLAR: THE MYSTERY BEHIND WHAT DRIVES ALL OF OUR ACTIONS

We are all unique and different in so many ways, but this next principle is what unites all of us. Regardless of what religion you are, where you were born, your skin color, height, weight, or gender, this principle is the driving factor in all of us. It is the one thing that guides every decision we make, whether it's done consciously or subconsciously.

This universal attribute is known as the **Pleasure-Pain Principle**. What the principle states is:

Everything we do is either to move toward things that make us feel good or away from things that make us feel bad.

We'll start with a very simple example of the principle, and then we'll go into much deeper levels of how it applies to you and the choices you make. We all want happiness in our lives, so if we were hungry and saw a delicious, free sandwich, we would move toward it. Hunger makes us unhappy; therefore, a tasty sandwich would satiate us, and that would make us happy.

On the flip side, we all want to avoid things that make us feel bad (pain). If a crazy man wearing a hockey mask swinging a chainsaw were running in your direction, you would move away from him, right? I should hope so! No rocket science yet right?

Well, don't worry, it doesn't get that much more complicated. Every single one of us wants to feel good. It's as basic as that. We take actions and make decisions because we hope they will bring us toward pleasure or away from pain. So our decision making process is based on what makes us feel good.

But the funny thing about it is we expect things to give us the most happiness. Where did we get that idea? Because you know what? All the things you want in life... you really don't want them.

Could everything you thought you knew be wrong?

YOU DON'T REALLY WANT THE CAR AND THE MONEY (HUH!?!)

If I said I were taking you to a car dealership right now to buy you any car you wanted and it won't cost you a dime, you'd probably be okay with that. But the truth is you really don't want the car. If I said I were going to give you a million dollars, you'd probably be pretty okay with that too. But you really don't want the money.

Now before you write me off as crazy, hear me out. You don't want a million dollars. Why would anybody just want a stack of green paper with pictures of dead presidents on them? But that stack of green paper can buy you a lot of nice things, can **help your family live a better life**, can help you attain your dreams and goals, and it can help you better the world.

What money BUYS is the "why" you want it.

In Tony Robbins' course *Get the Edge*, he explains we really don't want any of the things we think we want. What we really want is the *feeling* those things will give us. Why do you want that brand new dream car? Because it will give you status and make you feel really cool. Why do you want more money? Because it will make you feel free and successful. So what we are truly going after is never the thing, but the feeling that thing will give us.

Our ultimate goal is to improve our emotional state to simply feel better.

Our mind connects having that new car with feeling successful. So what drives us is the feeling we attach to things, not necessarily the things themselves. We condition ourselves to believe we first must have X before we can feel Y. In other words, once I have a million dollars, then I will feel like my life has worth. It's not the money we really want but the feeling of worthiness (by the way, to build a strong self-worth reread The Second Pillar starting on page 59.)

Are you getting this? Our goal is to start creating as much joy as we can in our lives.

WHOA! SLOW DOWN AND DON'T GET IT TWISTED

So you may be saying to yourself right now, "SWEET! He just said happiness is the best thing, and feeling good is what it's all about. Awesome! I'm going to go drink, smoke, and party like a rock star! WOOOO! Yeah, this book has given me the excuse I needed to act a fool."

Let's be clear: that is NOT what I'm saying. Let me repeat that: it is *not* what I'm saying at all.

The problem most people face, unfortunately, is they have a **false understanding of what *true* happiness is**. The problem is most people don't find happiness in things that temporarily make us feel good but that are extremely destructive in the long term.

If I eat one cookie, it makes me happy. Yes, I believe in healthy living, but I love me a cookie every now and again... especially those Thin Mints the Girl Scouts sell. Mmmm. (Sorry, I got lost in a memory.)

But have you ever eaten an entire package of cookies? They may taste good going down, but you probably felt pretty gross afterwards. You can only eat but so many cookies before you hit the coma-inducing "I Can't Eat One More Cookie" point. So clearly something like junk food can't bring ultimate happiness, even though in the short term it makes us feel good.

Other people searching for happiness turn to drugs and alcohol. In the short term, these drugs seem desirable because of the temporary euphoric feeling they give their users. But any rational person can see the horrific effects these drugs have on the human body and mind over time. I don't know about you, but I've never seen a crackhead I wanted to be like. I've never seen an alcoholic I would want to model. Over time, drugs and alcohol literally destroy our bodies and minds, so using these false stimulants cannot be the greatest happiness.

A physical pleasure cannot be the greatest form of happiness.

And yes, that includes ALL forms of physical pleasure (I think you know where I'm going with this).

WHAT IS THE GREATEST FEELING OF HAPPINESS?

By definition, the greatest feeling of happiness can never make you feel bad. So the greatest pleasure that you could ever bring into your life, is not smoking, drinking, eating, or anything like that. The ultimate pleasure is being part of and contributing to a larger community, something greater than yourself.

Have you ever been to a live professional sports event, like an NFL game, before? It's an experience like nothing else. But why in the world would anyone want to go to a game live? Think about it.

At a live game, it could be snowing wildly, causing people to huddle together freezing their tails off! But in your house, you've got climate control. You can make it as warm or as cool as you like. At a live game, a $2 hot dog will cost you about $8 bucks, a $1 drink might run you $10 bucks! In your house, you have a comfy couch, but at the game you are hunched over on a bleacher without proper back support. At home you get to see all the angles of the game perfectly with instant replay, and you can listen to commentators help guide you along the game. Everything you need and more is in your home... so why in the world would anyone want to actually go to a live event?!?!

It's the energy of being there, that's why. When you are at the game, you are surrounded by thousands of other people who are rooting for the team with you. You are part of something massive, and electricity is in the air. It's amazing to be part of 50,000 people doing "the wave," yelling at the opposing team, and high-fiving each other when you are winning.

When the team wins, you win, we all win. So it's worth it. It's worth the long drive, the cold, the overpriced ticket, and the overpriced food. It's all worth it to be there live, part of a larger community.

This applies on a larger and smaller level too. Would you want to play and win the championship game with none of your family or friends with you, or would you rather win the championship game with all of your closest family members and friends in the audience rooting you on? That's a no-brainer, isn't it? We all have a unique desire and want to **share our experiences** with those around us. We are social creatures by nature.

ISOLATION EQUALS UNHAPPINESS

If you have ever felt depressed or sad (and yes, we all have at some point), then you probably have isolated yourself from those around you. When you start feeling a little unhappy or you are feeling detached, you're most likely moving away from being a part of something. Isolation can lead to depression faster than anything else. Why do you think they put the hardest of criminals in solitary confinement while they are in prison? Being lonely is akin to torture.

When we get stressed out about life, we often choose to detach ourselves from others in an attempt to feel better. However, prolonged isolation will eventually make us feel worse. It is okay to spend some time alone, and sometimes it is the best thing to do. But you must make sure you don't spend so much time alone you forget how to function normally in society.

That is why it is so important to **get involved in activities on campus**. Becoming a student leader, volunteering your time, or joining a social club like a fraternity/sorority is extremely important to help you feel fulfilled and happy in your collegiate career.

You don't have to believe me right now, but I challenge you to test me by asking a question that will prove this is true. Find someone on campus who is having a blast, who is living the best life he or she possibly can, and ask that person this question: **"What groups are you involved with on campus?"** I'll bet that person rattles off an entire list of things he or she is part of on campus and in the community.

Then find someone who is having a horrible time in college and who just hates everything. Ask that person the very same question: **"What groups are you involved with on campus?"** I'm pretty confident that person will respond by saying he or she is not involved with anything; everything sucks, so that is why he or she doesn't join anything.

The bottom line is this: for you to begin your journey to success in the right way, you have to feel fulfilled. You start this process by getting involved with groups that give back, be it through community service, fundraising, education, and the like.

Many people will agree they enjoy **helping others**. It is something that offers a universal feeling of true happiness. You can never get sick of seeing the joy on someone's face that you helped; you will never have that gross feeling of eating an entire carton of cookies when you help someone. And if you have been reading this far into the book, that means you are truly dedicated to creating success and happiness in your life, so I'll give you a bonus right now.

The secret to wealth is providing value to other people's lives. The more value you give to others' lives, the more you will get in return, and money will be a byproduct of the value you add to others. If you are good at making a difference, you won't have to worry about making a dollar.

▸ GET IN THE HABIT OF WANTING TO HELP OTHERS

It is a known principle of success that if you help others get what they want, you will get what you want. It starts from wanting to truly help others for the sole purpose of helping. If you want to have a really great experience in college, and not just a normal experience, you need to get involved in something. It's not just about what the group can give you; it's also about what you can give to it.

What will you do to make your campus and your local community better than before you attended?

Giving and helping others provides meaning in your life. If you want to know whether your life has had meaning when it's all said and done, don't measure it by the number of dollars in your bank account. Measure it by the number of **people's lives that are better off because you existed**.

▸ THE BIGGEST MISTAKE PEOPLE WILL MAKE WITH THE PAIN-PLEASURE PRINCIPLE

But wait, what about those people who give to the point of burnout? If all I do is give and give, won't I get worn out, tired, and stressed? As I teach in my seminar **"The Secrets of Exceptional Student Leaders,"** you have to make sure you are not drawing water from an empty well. To give fully, you must first have something to give. You probably have heard of the saying "It is better to give than to receive." That saying has been altered over time from the original statement. If you trace that adage back to its origins, you'll find the proverb actually says "It's better to be in a position to give, than a position to receive." Changes your whole concept of the phrase, doesn't it?

Too much giving doesn't make you feel bad; it's the taking from yourself when you have nothing to give that makes you feel bad. Trying to spend five days straight with no sleep and no food so you can volunteer your time to help the homeless is noble, but foolish. You and I are humans, and we have needs that have to be met. As you start your journey to success, giving will bring you the greatest joy in the world. But the knowledge that to give, **you must first *have* something to give** is the true key to unlocking this pillar's potential.

And while you should always give to others, be sure to give to yourself as well. Many times it's much easier to give to others before we give to ourselves, but there is **nothing selfish about making sure you are well taken care of**. You are the only person responsible for yourself, as we talked about in the First Pillar. Therefore, if you haven't joined a group or created something personally fulfilling yet, now is the time to start.

Believe me, you can contribute more to the world than you have already. It's amazing how much we can stretch ourselves if we need to. Just remember that if you stretch a rubber band too far, it will eventually snap.

LEARNING, NOT JUST READING

To get the most from this chapter, take a moment to do the following Action Steps:

1) If you are not involved in an organization yet, resolve to join something by the end of this month.

2) If you are involved in an organization, brainstorm how you can provide more value to the group.

3) Schedule at least one community service activity into your calendar this semester.

PERSONAL REFLECTION

1) What did I learn from this?

2) How can I apply this principle to my life?

3) What specifically will I do today to apply this principle to my life?

CHAPTER SEVEN

THE FIFTH PILLAR: THE SINGLE MOST IMPORTANT DETERMINING FACTOR TO YOUR CONTINUED SUCCESS

"You will never catch an eagle flying with seagulls."
-Arel Moodie

Do you want to know the single most important determining factor to your continued success in school and in life? You can have all of the ingredients to be wildly successful on the inside—all of the knowledge and skills—but this external factor could lead to more chaos and destruction than you can handle. All of the previous pillars can be destroyed if this one pillar of success is not properly attended to. The Fifth Pillar is "**The Average of 5**," which states:

You are going to be the average of the five people you spend the most time with.

My best friend and former business partner Bert Gervais introduced me to the idea that if you're hanging out with five knuckleheads, you are going to be the average knucklehead, and if you're hanging out with five millionaires, you're probably going to be an average millionaire. Who you spend the majority of your time with will reflect how quickly or how slowly you move toward success. **The people around you will either motivate you or drag you down**; they will support you or cause you to fail.

Those surrounding you will greatly influence everything you do.

THE PROOF IS IN THE PUDDING (OR I GUESS IN THIS CASE, THE GPA)

Still need some more proof you will be the average of the five people you spend the most time with? Try this little exercise on for size, and I bet you will be astounded.

- Take out a piece of paper and write down the names of the five friends you spend the most time with who are students.
- Find out what their GPAs are and write them next to their names.
- Add up all of the GPAs, then divide that sum by five.
- The result? I bet that number is right around where your GPA is.

Go ahead, test it out. This equation works with a lot of other things too. **The amount of money** you make is probably about the average of the five people you spend the most time with. If the five people you hang out with the most don't take school seriously, you probably won't take school seriously. If the five people you hang around with the most are on the dean's list, you are probably on the **dean's**

list. If the five people you hang around with work out regularly, you probably **work out regularly**.

Your goal is to find the people on the wavelength you want to be on. You have to be true to yourself. If you are a vegan, it will be hard for you to hang with a bunch of hunters. Because eventually you would have to go out and shoot Bambi! How would you feel about yourself at that point?

TRYING TO FIT A ROUND PEG IN A SQUARE HOLE

Growing up, I spent too much of my time trying to fit in, trying to be someone I wasn't. You may know what that feels like too, as I've found a lot of people have dealt with this challenge. I can vividly remember the night before my first day of college: I felt such trepidation and excitement about attending college. Would college finally be the answer to my prayers? Would I fit in? Would I be cool or just a loser all over again?

Sitting there in my room packing my clothes, I remember looking up and glancing at my reflection in the mirror and locking eyes with myself. I looked into my eyes and promised myself I would be willing to grow to become the man I wanted to be. And at the time, the man I wanted to be was just someone who was accepted. So whatever I had to do to be cool, I was going to do.

When I got into college, I met a group of guys who were all definitely cool and popular. I figured when you first meet people, they can't tell if you are cool or not, so I would sneak my way in under the radar and just kind of be the satellite friend. I was lucky to have a roommate all the girls liked and all the guys wanted to be like, and he brought me along whenever he would hang out. I felt I was now cool through association.

Everything was good except for the fact that a lot of the new cool people I was hanging out with drank and smoked weed a lot. That was never my thing. I tried hanging out with them while everyone else was stoned and drunk and I was the only sober person, and I remember not wanting to seem like a loser (and thinking I needed to get messed up too because being sober and hanging around drunk people isn't fun at all), so I decided to give in to peer pressure. It seemed like this was the only way to finally get what I thought I wanted, which was to be cool and have a bunch of friends.

Drinking underage and smoking weed were not things I would have been proud to tell the world I was doing. In fact, if you want the simplest way to know whether what you are doing is right or wrong, just ask yourself this simple yet powerful question:

"If what I am about to do were to be put on the front page of every newspaper and on every website for everyone and my mama to see, would I be okay with that or would I feel ashamed?"

That one question alone will completely change your life for the better, even if that is all you take from this book (remember the power of the slight edge?).

The real challenge to living a shameful lifestyle is called our conscience. It's the little voice that helps us know what's right and what's wrong. I call it our "internal pitchfork." We have an internal vibration inside of us that lets us know what is good and what is bad. And my internal pitchfork kept going off like crazy saying "WARNING, WARNING" because what I was doing was not consistent with the real image I wanted for myself.

I wanted to be cool, but I didn't want to sacrifice my personal beliefs of what I was sure was right. My internal pitchfork kept telling me what I was doing was not right.

What's funny is the more I tried to fit in, the more I felt like I didn't want to fit in. I wasn't happy. I was trying to be someone and something I wasn't. One night when I was hanging out with everyone while they were drinking and smoking, I looked around and asked myself, "Are these the people I really want to be like?" Would I feel proud being on the front page of every newspaper showing me drinking and smoking? The answer was no.

I felt really conflicted because I wasn't happy hanging out with the cool kids, and I wouldn't be happy if I weren't cool. What was I to do? I wanted to be accepted, but what I didn't understand back then was the rule of three.

THE RULE OF 3: YOU REALLY ONLY GET UP TO THREE FRIENDS WHEREVER YOU GO

The rule of three states that in whatever situation you enter, high school, college, summer camp, a job, internship, and so forth, you'll be lucky if you stay in touch with more than three people from that situation.

Think about it. How many people do you still keep in touch with from elementary school? Junior high school? High school? And not just a random Facebook message or saying "hi" if you happen to be in the same place at the same time, but true friends you will call on the phone to just talk with or you will plan to go somewhere with to chill outside of the normal setting in which you would ordinarily see them. If that number is really small, congratulations, you are cool.

No matter how cool or uncool we *think* we are, if we just have one person, just one person we connect with, then we are cool because that is as good as anyone else has it. This concept of "cool" becomes more and more a myth the older you get.

BEWARE OF ENERGY PARASITES

As you decide who to spend most of your time with, beware of those who will sabotage you. Right now in your life, there are people who probably are toxic to your journey toward success. I call them Energy Parasites or EPs. Every time you are around these people, they suck your energy dry. They do it through their **pessimistic view** of the world and their desire for their problems to be your problems.

Everything seems to always be in chaos for them, and they want to make sure you are in the same chaos. Energy Parasites are the people who are quick to shoot down your dreams and the first ones to find what's wrong with a situation instead of what's right. They are the people who will make you feel like you can't accomplish your goals.

Have you ever had a friend like that? When an EP calls you, your first thought after looking at the caller ID is "Damn! I really don't want to take this call." Every time you share good news with an EP, he or she looks for a way to rain on your parade. Tell an EP you are excited you got a new job, and the EP says, "Well, make sure not to mess up like you did at your previous job." No matter what is going right, an EP will find something wrong.

And the EP always wants to burden you with his or her problem, and it's probably not even a big deal. EPs will call you crying and screaming because their shoelaces are untied! The littlest things set them off.

Who needs it?

WHY PEOPLE WANT TO HOLD YOU DOWN

If you find someone who believes he or she is perfect and the whole world is the problem, that is a good sign you are dealing with an EP. If everywhere that person goes there is a problem, there is good chance they are actually the problem.

Have you ever seen crabs in a barrel? You can put live crabs in a barrel without a lid and not worry about any of the crabs escaping. Why? Because if one does try to climb out, another crab will be there to pull it back down. A lot of people are just like those crabs in the barrel. But why would someone choose to be an EP? Why would anyone want to be a crab in a barrel? Well, most of the time, EPs do not realize they are EPs.

The deep psychological reason why others hate to see you succeed is because if you succeed and they don't, you'll serve as a reminder about their untapped potential. You will show them they have no excuse not to succeed, and they don't want that because it is a lot easier for them to not try and complain why they don't have anything than it is to take action in their life. By seeing you fail, they can feel good about themselves. This is the only way for them to feel important. EPs will be your downfall if you choose to consistently subject yourself to their psychological assault.

LIBERATING YOURSELF FROM ENERGY PARASITES

As you begin your journey to success, you have to be around people who will support you and will move you in the right direction. As W. Clement Stone says in his book *The Success System That Never Fails*,

"You are subject to your environment. Therefore, select the environment that will best develop you toward your desired objective."

What that means is you are going to have to fire some people from your life to create the best environment for your success. That may sound harsh, but it's true, and I want to help save you years of stress, heartache, and pain. To start achieving your goals and dreams, you have to get rid of the deadweight that is going to hold you down. You have to get rid of the "friends" who will try to make you drink instead of study: those who will have you do activities that don't represent who you are or who you want to be.

The good news is you don't have to invite the people you will be firing from your life into a boardroom Donald Trump-style and yell, "YOU'RE FIRED!" And you don't have to completely eliminate anyone from your life who you may truly love but now realize is toxic to your well-being.

Firing an EP does not mean you don't love that person or think you are better than him or her. It just means that if that person wants to have a messed up life, that's not your problem. **You have complete control over who you choose to spend the most time with.**

Choose to spend more of your time with people who support you and who you want to be like, and less time with EPs.

OKAY, BUT HOW DO I ACTUALLY DO IT?

There is no single way to start firing EPs from your life, but this one technique has been very helpful for many people, and I'm 100% confident it will work for you too. Instead of making it obvious you do not want to spend time with these EPs anymore (because that can be very socially awkward), simply choose to **fill your time with activities that involve the people you want to be around** and the activities that move you forward.

Here's an example. You are ready to begin your journey to success, and you identify that building your leadership skills will help you in your endeavors. So you join a club that does community service on weekends. When your EPs invite you to do something wrong like drinking or smoking, you can easily say, "I'd love to, but I have to be up in the morning to go volunteer at the soup kitchen. Hey, do you want to come with me?"

One of two things will happen.

The EPs will change their attitude and want to be part of all of the new things you are doing. Or they will stop hanging around you, and you will be free. By the way, another reason you ask them to come with you is due to something called the law of reciprocity. Because you said no to them, by giving them a chance to reciprocate and say no to you, it allows you to turn someone down with no one's feelings getting hurt.

Deciding to fire people who are sucking the life out of you is definitely not the easiest choice to make, especially when the EP in your life might be **a family member or a loved one** (yeah, I know that one is rough). But remember, what's hard is often what's the most fulfilling.

So if you find your EPs are family members, be there to support them and love them as best you can. **Just share your goals and dreams with someone else.**

▸ USE "THE LIST"

Here is an **action step** you should take right now. This is going to be a tough one, so you may want to do it alone where you can feel safe and open with yourself and not worry about people wondering what you are writing.

Make a list of the people you spend the most time with. Next to their names, you will add a plus sign, "+," or a minus sign, "-". The plus sign represents people who have values similar to yours or values that motivate you to move forward in life—those people who are supportive and those you know will help you on your journey to success. They add value to your life. Put a minus sign next to those who fall under the category of EPs. These are the people who you feel aren't helping you along your journey of success. Keep spending time with the people with pluses, and start distancing yourself from the people with minuses.

This can be **very emotional and very hard to do**, so I recommend doing it when you have a free afternoon or don't have to worry about having to do anything in particular for a few hours. Again, it may be tough for you, but it will be one of the best decisions you make for your overall sanity.

› HOW DO I FIND THE RIGHT PEOPLE TO BE AROUND?

Now that you have made The List and have figured out who you need to spend less time with, you may be wondering how you can find the right people to be around if they are not currently in your life. You should start looking for new people who will add value to your life and make you step out of your comfort zone to grow as a person.

So where can you find these people? Here are a few recommendations:

- Fraternities/Sororities
- Student Leadership Groups
- Professional Associations
- Orientation Leaders
- Executive Boards of Student Groups
- Pre-Professional Organizations

Students are told to get involved on campus for a very specific reason: because there **is a correlation between students who get involved on campus and those who succeed academically** and as professionals. If you are involved in a student group, take a leadership role. If you are not involved yet, get involved with something.

It doesn't matter what you do, just do something!

A good place to start is with your interests. What is it you like to do? Another question to ask is who is the type of person you want to be? Do a Google search with that interest and the name of your city or town. Or you can go to your Student Activities Office and get a list of the organizations that exist on campus. You will be amazed at what you can find.

› FIND A MENTOR

Finding a mentor is a huge key to success. Tapping into the brain of someone who has already been there and done that and wants to help you is an amazing way to start surrounding yourself with **positive influences**. Every single successful person you have ever heard of most likely had a mentor. A mentor could be a family member, a friend, teacher, or maybe even someone you have never met, but you've read their books before.

Mentors serve as your compass on this journey. They can see the mistakes you might make before you make them, and they can help you when you just need someone to talk to. Mentors help you become the best you that you can be.

I hope you consider me a mentor, and I'd love to help you in any way I can. Please feel free to stay in touch with me. You can find my most up to date contact information at **www.arelmoodie.com**.

ADVANCED LEARNING

If you want to learn a really cool technique to recruiting really successful people you have NO connections to as your mentor, go to **www.yourstartingpointonline.com**.

There, you will learn the same technique I learned from my mentors, neither of whom I knew before I contacted them: a millionaire and a young entrepreneur who is a best-selling author.

You will succeed or fail based on who you let into your inner circle. You will become the average of the five people you spend the most time with. Your time is the most precious asset you have because you can never get it back. Make sure you are investing your time wisely in yourself and others.

▸ LEARNING, NOT JUST READING

To get the most from this chapter, take a moment to do the following Action Steps:

1) Plan some time to go through "The List" exercise.

2) Write down all of the qualities and attributes your "best self" will have. Once you have this list, start aligning your actions with the people who surround you to foster these attributes.

3) Brainstorm a list of people you would want to mentor you. And set up a time you will contact them either by email or phone.

4) If you are not involved in a student group, get involved in one within the next two weeks.

▸ PERSONAL REFLECTION

1) What did I learn from this?

2) How can I apply this principle to my life?

3) What specifically will I do today to apply this principle to my life?

CHAPTER EIGHT

ARE YOU READY?

THE TOOLS WON'T WORK UNLESS YOU USE THEM

What you've just read are your tools to create your starting point for student success. But the tools won't work unless you use them. A hammer lying on the floor can't do anything by itself, but in the right hands, it can help build a home. The hammer is useless unless it is used. That is why this book is your starting point for success.

This book gives you a new lens to see your life through. I hope you are ready to take the journey to success and do something every day to become better than yesterday, whether it's reading, taking action, or stopping activities that are unproductive in your life.

And here's another success principle you can add to your war chest:

Pareto Principle 80/20 Rule
The Pareto Principle states that roughly
80% of the effects come from 20% of the cause.

Another way to think of this is to say the results we achieve are the result of about 20% (and sometimes less!) of the stuff we do.

In our case, the 80% is you taking the time to read this book. It has taken you time and focus to spend time learning about these life-changing pillars of success. The 20% represents your application of these principles to your life. The 20% is making that one uncomfortable phone call—it's the action it takes to move you toward the goals you want to achieve. Just reading this books means absolutely nothing unless you actively apply the principles to your life.

This book wasn't created just to be a form of entertainment (however, I do hope you've enjoyed spending some time with me). This book was meant to **change your mindset** and help you to take the necessary steps forward in life and in school, right now. If you just wanted to veg out, your time would have been better spent looking up stupid videos on YouTube.

But since you've come this far (assuming you just didn't skip ahead to this part!), **you are a person of action and greatness**—and not of future greatness, by the way. You are great right now, in this moment. Not just great... you're awesome!

Completing this book serves as a milestone along your journey. It's a point of reference so you can say: "This is my starting point. Today, I am in control of my life. Yes, I am successful. Yes, I am an awesome student. Yes, I am smart. Yes, I will start today truly living the life I know I deserve and I demand from myself."

We started with a congratulations, and I'd like to end with one, too.

Congratulations! The real fun starts now, wherever you are in this journey called life. The satisfaction is in fulfilling your dreams, goals, and aspirations. The fun is in the work it takes to live as the true success you know you already are.

AND YES, IT'S POSSIBLE FOR YOU

You can do this: you can be more successful than you have ever dreamed of. It's possible for you to achieve your goals and wildest dreams. You have to start stretching outside your comfort zone and do the things others won't so you can have the things others don't.

There is a great three-step process to achieving a goal that you want, and here it is:

- **Step 1: See someone who did it.**
- **Step 2: Believe you can do it.**
- **Step 3: Commit to doing it (then actually do it!).**

As fitness guru Tony Little says, **"See It, believe It, achieve It."**

It's simple but powerful, as most things are in this world. Whatever another person can achieve, so can you. So if someone you admire has achieved success as a student or as a person, it's possible for you to achieve that same or greater success. You just have to believe it's possible. Nothing can ever happen until you can first see it in your mind. It's called having a vision.

And finally, you must commit to doing it. How do you know you've truly committed to your success? It's very simple. Your commitment to something can be measured by one thing, and one thing only: action.

Commit to your goals by taking action so you can achieve them.

The journey may not be easy and it may be long, but it will be worth doing every step of the way.

▸ YES, IT DOES TAKE TIME

You're in the home stretch. You're almost done, and you're just about ready to properly begin your journey to success in the most effective way possible. However, please understand that

Success is a journey, not a destination.

You will go through many failures and setbacks and at first feel like you just aren't cut out to make it. It's normal. Everyone reacts to change that way. You just have to walk through the fire, get over the hump, and knock down the obstacles. My mentor once told me **every "overnight" success takes at least five to seven years**. Most people will never see all of the hard work and self-discipline that goes into becoming someone of great substance and character, but it's there!

You are on the journey of a lifetime, and though I may not be able to predict the length of your life, if you stay on the path you started with this book, I'm sure you will be able to have a depth to your life many people will wish for. **You are more powerful than you know**, and I wish you true success and happiness in this lifetime.

The ball has been passed to you now. What are you going to do with it? What **specifically** are you going to do RIGHT NOW that will move you toward your goals?

Make this minute **Your Starting Point**. Begin by applying the principles in this book to your life until they become part of you. Your next step is to continue to invest in yourself, to learn, and to grow.

ADVANCED READING

You can go to **www.yourstartingpointonline.com** for a list of other recommended readings as well as to sign up for our free Starting Point for Student Success newsletter to get the info you need to keep you on path during your journey.

One last thought before we go: this journey isn't really about trying to find out who you will become. It is about discovering who you already are.

In the immortal words of Dr. Martin Luther King Jr.:

"Take the first step in faith. You don't have to see the whole staircase, just take the first step."

To Your Success!

Arel Moodie

PS: You're awesome!

BIBLIOGRAPHY

Eker, T. Harv. *Secrets of the Millionaire Mind: Marketing the Inner Game of Wealth*. New York: HarperCollins, 2005.

Gerber, Michael E. *The E-Myth Revisited: Why Most Small Businesses Don't Work and What to Do About It*. New York: HarperCollins, 1995.

Hartgill, David. "Power of Compounding." *The Advertiser*. September 15, 1997.

Hill, Napoleon. *Think and Grow Rich*. New York: Penguin, 2003.

Hoffer, Eric. *The True Believer: Thoughts on the Nature of Mass Movements*. New York: HarperCollins, 2002.

Olson, Jeff. "The Slight Edge Philosophy." http://www.topachievement.com/slightedge.html.

Ray, James Arthur. *The Secret*. TS Production Ltd. DVD.

Robbins, Anthony. Anthony Robbins—Great Inspirational Leader. Guthy Renker. Compact disc.

"Sibling Rivalry: Comparison." Public Broadcasting System. http://pbskids.org/itsmylife/family/sibrivalry/article5.html.

Stone, W. Clement. *The Success System That Never Fails*. Englewood Cliffs: Prentice Hall, 1962.

Tolle, Eckhart. *The Power of Now: A Guide to Spiritual Enlightenment.* Novato: New World, 2004.

Tracy, Brian. *Time Power: A Proven System for Getting More Done in Less Time Than You Ever Thought Possible.* New York: AMACOM, 2007.

WHO IS AREL MOODIE?

SPEAKER - AUTHOR - ENTREPRENEUR

Featured in *USA Today* and *Young Money magazine* and on ABC, NBC, and Fox News affiliates, Arel Moodie is an expert on helping this generation of students start taking action toward their goals like true professionals. Arel is living proof that no matter what your background is, we all can live the lives we deserve.

From starting his life on welfare in the projects of Brooklyn, New York, witnessing those around him being murdered and imprisoned, to becoming president of four college organizations, working in corporate America, and starting two businesses, including www.arelmoodie.com, Arel's stories about his victories over self-defeating behavior and environmental obstacles have captured the hearts of students across the country.

As a professional speaker, Arel has spoken to over 50,000 students in 37 states and two countries—all before his 25th birthday. It's no wonder why he is named one of the Country's Top Generation Y Leaders in the book *Millennial Leaders* and is featured in the book *Student Entrepreneurs—Graduating With a Profit.*

Always the entertainer, Arel likes to dance and has opened for the Grammy Award-winning R&B group 112.

LIST OF SPEAKING ENGAGEMENTS

To book Arel, contact us at 877-803-4221 or e-mail us at info@arelmoodie.com.

‣ THE COLLEGE SUCCESS PROGRAM

(Based on Arel's 5 Pillars of Success discussed in *Your Starting Point For Student Success*)

Let's face it. Going through college can be challenging—and it's not surprising students get lost in the process.

Arel's mission with this program is to stop that from happening and empower students to achieve the greatest possible results both in school and in life.

From this program, students will learn how to create powerful lives for themselves and understand why college is so important in helping them reach their goals. College students will learn how to thrive during and after college. No matter their age, students will discover how to move forward to create the life of their dreams with a blueprint we call the "Life Intention Plan."

Students exposed to this program not only perform better academically, but they are also happier and better able to manage a challenging collegiate environment.

THE SECRETS OF EXCEPTIONAL STUDENT LEADERS: FROM STUDENT LEADER TO STUDENT CEO

Did you know almost every great business, political, and social leader developed his or her skills during college or high school? For instance, both Tony Robbins and Donald Trump were student leaders. It's absolutely crucial to foster young leaders and equip them with the skills they need to not just survive but also thrive in the 21st century.

Being a student leader can be tough when you don't have the skills you need to succeed. We have developed this special program to help students take their leadership skills to the next level.

Your student leaders will learn:

- The biggest mistake most leaders make and how to avoid it
- How to turn "dead weight" members into productive, motivated members
- How to throw events people will want to attend and how to get rave reviews
- The secret psychology of great leaders that will make people want to follow you

This extremely powerful presentation is a must-see for your student leaders!

‣ TURNING YOUR PASSION INTO YOUR PROFESSION: HOW TO FIND YOUR PASSION AND GET PAID TO DO IT!

In a world where almost everybody hates what they're doing at work, this program has never been more important.

In just one presentation, your students will discover the secret formula to identifying their unique strengths and passions as well as how to turn them into a rewarding and fulfilling career.

Some side effects of this presentation are a massive increase in school attendance, better grades, higher school morale, and improved graduation rates. When students get a vision of how everything they are learning relates to their lives, a newfound energy and drive follows, ensuring their success.

Using a systematic process, Arel will show your students the most direct roadmap to turning their passions into their professions.

DYNAMIC PUBLIC SPEAKING FOR STUDENT LEADERS

Public speaking skills are no longer optional: they are very much a crucial part of leadership in the 21st century, as demonstrated so well by our nation's 44th president.

Students leave this presentation knowing how to present their views charismatically, regardless of their current speaking skill level. Not only will they master communication, but they'll also see their self-esteem, confidence, and persuasiveness skyrocket.

Your student leaders will learn:

- How to capture an audience's attention immediately with the two most effective opening techniques

- How to utilize platform skills that demonstrate confidence and professionalism

- The quickest and most effective way to overcome stage fright

- The tightly held secret to keeping your audience engaged the entire time

If your students need to become better presenters or speak at an upcoming event, you can't afford to miss this presentation.

HOW WILL YOU BE REMEMBERED? AS A WARNING OR AS AN EXAMPLE?

Would you like to have a presentation that builds bonds among racial lines, motivates students toward success, and teaches them about their country's past and present great leaders of color while helping them develop a clear vision for their lives?

This is not just some boring history lecture—it's a way for students from all backgrounds to connect with the ideas of our great leaders from the past and present to help inspire their thoughts and actions.

There are only two types of people in the world: Warnings and Examples.

Students leave this program understanding why their time on this earth is important and how they can best become an example for themselves, their families, and their campus communities. If you want your students to know anything is possible if they set their minds to it and start taking action today, then you need to bring this program onto your campus.

› WANT TO CONTINUE YOUR JOURNEY?

www.yourstartingpointonline.com was created to give you more information about beginning your journey to success that could not be fit in this book.

To get great valuable information guaranteed to help you achieve more in less time go to **www.yourstartingpointonline.com** now and sign up!